HAMILTON COUNTY FOOD

From Casual Grub to Gastropubs

Karen Kennedy

AMERICAN PALATE

Published by American Palate
A Division of The History Press
Charleston, SC
www.historypress.net

Front cover, clockwise from top left: The shakshuka at Carmel's Eggshell Bistro—a Moroccan dish of tomato, onion, garlic, kale and blistered cherry tomatoes topped with a baked hen's egg and chèvre and accompanied by a grilled baguette. *Courtesy of Larry Hanes*; Summer's bounty of fresh, juicy peaches from a Hamilton County Farmer's Market! *Photo by author*; Patachou's Martha Hoover. *Photo provided*; Breaded tenderloin sandwich, smoked wings, tacos and the manly wedge salad from Four Day Ray in Fishers. *Photo provided*; Locally brewed Big Lug beer is featured at Sahm's Ale House in Carmel. *Photo provided.*
Back cover: A rendering of the fondly remembered Blue Ribbon Dairy Drive-In as created by Noblesville artist Rodney Reveal. *Courtesy of Rodney Reveal*; *inset*: Bub's Big Ugly Burger—to date, only four people have finished it. *Photo provided.*

First published 2019

Manufactured in the United States

ISBN 9781467139625

Library of Congress Control Number: 2019932627

This book is dedicated to those who serve us food and drink. It's an often thankless job, but I, for one, am thankful. I did it for many years. My feet still hurt. You rule.

Also, to my mom, Lorraine Altenhof, who never met a stranger. She taught me to see the good in everyone I met, and that helps a lot when you're in the restaurant business. She also taught me that I could do anything I set my mind to—you know, like writing a book. And, lord, how she loved a party. I'm sure she's serving bourbon slush and party mix in heaven right now.

CONTENTS

FOREWORD

Although Hamilton County has deep agricultural roots, the "local foods" movement here didn't always mean what it does today. Certainly, people here have always eaten what was nearby whether it was a favorite pork tenderloin sandwich at a downtown Noblesville bar, fresh berries from a local you-pick farm or crispy battered fish at a local fish fry. And the annual midsummer 4-H Fair is eagerly anticipated as a way to enjoy food that harkens back to memories of our childhood, like elephant ears and funnel cakes.

But as these suburban Indianapolis communities grew through the years, their palates also grew. It was as if there were two Hamilton Counties: the one that harkened back to its farm days and the one that yearned to grow in sophistication. Brave chefs, restaurateurs and entrepreneurs recognized this yearning and blazed a culinary trail through Hamilton County, bringing new flavors to a dining public that was clamoring for culinary adventure and committed to supporting those who live and work in their own communities. Finally, in Hamilton County, the farm (which was there all along) has truly come to the table.

In this book, Karen Kennedy explores the journey that Hamilton County food has taken from rather simple beginnings to the present day, in which Hamilton County has become a culinary and tourism destination unto itself (and a pretty great place to live, work and eat). Given her long history as both a restaurant person and a food writer, as well as a commitment to all things local, she is uniquely qualified to do so. I hope you devour this book and then go out and devour all the amazing food that Hamilton County has to offer.

Dig in.

Brenda Myers
President/CEO, Hamilton County Tourism

ACKNOWLEDGEMENTS

First and foremost, this book, as with everything else in my life these days, would not have been possible without Abby David, my beloved Peach. She was a research assistant extraordinaire, and her contributions to this book are immeasurable. My dining companion for many years now, she's explored all these restaurants with me and gallivanted all over the county with me taking pictures, taking bites and taking notes. She also does the dishes when I fall asleep immediately following dinner because I've been up writing since 4:00 a.m. All my love to you, Peach.

Many thanks are also due to Hamilton County historian David Heighway and Hamilton County Indiana Room librarian Nancy Massey (both fellow authors!). Also, big thanks to Katherine Dill and the team at the Carmel-Clay Historical Center, the staff of the Hamilton County Historical Society and the folks at the Westfield Washington Historical Society.

Much of the history of our restaurants here would have been lost without the efforts of Brad Cook, whose restaurant articles are sourced numerous times here. Also, a shout-out to Julia Spalding and *Indianapolis Monthly* magazine, which is another source of great restaurant history for Indianapolis and Hamilton County. In the 1970s, their food writers were forced to assess the relative merits of the black bean soup at Outback Steakhouse in order to fill the dining section. To see how far our culinary landscape has evolved is extraordinarily gratifying.

I'm incredibly grateful for the support from the Hamilton County Visitor's Bureau and the many citizens of Hamilton County who shared their memories with me. And I would be remiss if I failed to also call out the efforts of the many awesome food writers in Indianapolis who work each day to keep the culinary scene top-of-mind: Liz Biro of the *Indianapolis Star*, Jolene Ketzenberger of eatdrinkindy.com and Jennifer Rubinstein of *Edible Indy* magazine.

Many thanks to my editor, John Rodrigue, who was unfailingly supportive throughout this process, and to my amazing copy editor Sara Miller, whose eagle eye saved me a thousand embarrassments. And, of course, to the restaurateurs who have, over lo these many years, lent their blood, sweat and tears to the labor of feeding others.

INTRODUCTION

I come from the land of Jell-O® molds.

Growing up in Huntington, Indiana, my mother taught me from a very young age that food was love. (My hips are a testament to that!) She worked outside the home for a good portion of my childhood, and I was always proud that she was a strong, independent working woman. She was a telephone operator for "Ma Bell" when she met my dad at a dance at the Aragon Ballroom in Chicago. He was a handsome soldier just home from Germany after World War II, and she was just spunky enough to tell him "no" when he asked her to dance. They had a long and happy marriage.

Even though she worked, we had a home-cooked dinner every night. My mother (God rest her soul) loved to cook, and while I thought everything she put on the table was marvelous, I was in my late teens before I realized these universal food truths: green beans can come from something other than a Green Giant can, Jell-O® salad isn't really a salad, iceberg is not the only kind of lettuce, garlic comes in a form other than salt and there are more kinds of cheese in the world than American, Swiss and cheddar.

I have a very vivid recollection of being invited to a neighbor's home for dinner when I was about eight years old and being presented with a steamed artichoke with drawn butter as an appetizer. I was simultaneously thrilled and terrified. It was the most exotic thing I'd ever seen in my life. I had no idea how to go about eating it, so I looked busy with my water glass and watched everyone else until I learned the technique, and then I dove in. It was divine. That was the first time I realized that food could be more than sustenance—it could be spectacular.

I tried to tell my mom about how we should be having artichokes for dinner every night, but she was having none of it. We weren't quite as "fancy" as the neighbors, she reasoned, and why should she go to all the trouble of seeking out fresh artichokes at the store when we had several perfectly acceptable cans of green beans in the cabinet?

Throughout my college years, I continued to experiment with cooking. (Steamed broccoli was a game changer for me—who knew that a cooked vegetable could still require a knife to eat?) But it wasn't until I landed in Chicago and started working in a fine-dining restaurant that my eyes were really opened to all the magical things food could be. My mom would come and visit and would dutifully proclaim that the food at my restaurant was "good," but I could tell she still thought it was all a bit over the top. And when I cooked for her, she would watch with concern as I added ingredients she'd never considered, using tools she'd never seen before. (She always brought her own coffee when she came to visit because she didn't like my dark roast, and one morning I awoke to find her struggling to open her can of Folgers with my garlic press.)

I continued to work in the restaurant business for many more years. As a restless spirit, I had a hard time sitting still, and the restaurant business gave me everything I needed: social interaction, a fast-paced environment and the opportunity to serve beautiful and creative food. (The cold, hard cash wasn't bad, either.) Although I always worked in the dining room, I had mad, crazy respect for the cooks and chefs on the line. They were creating art on one plate after another, even when they were too tired to stand or so hot that a weaker soul would have passed out.

I live in Indianapolis now. I lived in New England for a while, but I'm a Hoosier through and through, and Indiana is my home. My days in the restaurant business are behind me. I've been lucky to be able to spend a fair amount of time abroad and on both coasts, and dining out is always central to my traveling experience. I believe that there's no better way to understand a place and a culture than to sit in a restaurant and observe both the food and the people who are serving it and eating it. In previous years, culinary trends began in Europe, made their way to our coasts and then worked their way inward, coming to the Midwest years after they had become passé everywhere else. But in recent years, I've seen that change. The Midwest has produced some amazing chefs who are driving a culinary revolution all their own, using ingredients unique to this corner of the world. I'm proud to be a Hoosier foodie, and I can't wait to see what comes next.

For hundreds of years, across the Midwest and around the world, food has been a way to bring people together, and restaurants have provided a vehicle for that much-needed social interaction. While breaking bread together, families connect, strangers become friends and those whose opinions differ may find some common ground. The folks who dedicate their lives to the restaurant business receive far less credit than they deserve—they put in long and hard hours for a profit margin that many entrepreneurs would consider paltry, they work on the weekends and the holidays (when the rest of us want to play) and they only eat after all of their customers have been fed. Then, they fall into bed and do it all again the next day. For them, it is truly a labor of love.

The history of a place cannot be fully told without telling the tales of the restaurateurs, and Hamilton County is no different. The American culinary scene evolved around here in much the same way it did across the country. From the taverns of the late 1800s and early 1900s, which offered comfort and (reportedly less than stellar) sustenance to weary travelers; the backdoor speakeasies of the Roaring Twenties; the supper clubs of the 1940s; the mom-and-pop diners, drive-ins and burger joints of the 1950s; the chains that symbolized progress and automation and the gourmet revolution of the 1970s and 1980s to the farm-to-table, locavore movements of today, those who opened their doors to strangers and put plates of food in front of them have helped shape our society. These are the places where couples went on first dates, became engaged and celebrated weddings and anniversaries, the places where workers shared drinks and commiserated about the changing economy and the job market, the places where citizens went to share their joy or outrage when elections were won or lost or current events changed the landscape of their lives. While we don't have the continuous documentation of today's selfies and "food porn" to chronicle their stories, we can—through menus, memories, clippings and snapshots—piece together a history of food's role in the development of our cities and towns and pay tribute to those who served it.

From a historical perspective, chains, franchises and fast-food restaurants are important because they influenced the culinary landscape (for better or worse), so they're included in the histories of restaurants in each city or town. However, none of these types of establishments are featured in the "can't-miss" sections in the later chapters (nor are small restaurant groups that are not based in Indiana). This book is solely a celebration of restaurants owned and operated by local people who are deeply entrenched in the communities they serve. Note: This cannot be an all-inclusive listing. There are myriad small, local restaurants that we were not able to include, although that doesn't mean they're not worth a visit. It just means that Hamilton County is bursting with unique and delightful independently owned restaurants, and there's neither room nor time to list them all. Instead, we feature the iconic restaurants that have stood the test of time as well as newer restaurants that are trailblazing and remarkable.

The work of feeding others is a labor of love for those who serve it. So it is with this book for me. I was in the trenches of the restaurant business for more than twenty years, and I know very well the rewards, joys, pains and satisfaction that come from having such an intimate perspective into people's lives and loves as you lean over them to put down a plate.

Indiana food came from humble beginnings, but it's certainly come a long way. We need to pay homage to those who forged the path with those early restaurants, because they have helped to shape the culinary landscape that we enjoy today. So, to everyone who has ever worked at or eaten in a restaurant (I think that covers every single one of us, yes?) I say…

Bon appétit.

1

FROM LONGHORN TO FOOD PORN

How Restaurants in America Came to Be

YOU'LL EAT IT AND YOU'LL LIKE IT: THE LATE 1700s

In the late 1700s and early 1800s, as territories were being settled, restaurants simply did not exist. As people moved into newly settled areas, they needed places to stay until they could build their own homes. This necessity birthed inns, which were bare-bones sleeping rooms. But, because these weary travelers arriving on horseback also had to eat, these early innkeepers also rustled up some pretty rudimentary grub. There was no semblance of a menu; the inn guests ate whatever was put in front of them and toddled off to bed. However, across the pond in Europe, restaurants and cafés were popping up at a rapid pace.

TRAINS, TAVERNS AND TIPPLERS: THE 1800s

As a result of the Industrial Revolution in the early 1800s, railroads slowly began to connect towns. As more folks moved from place to place, more folks needed food and lodging. The Monon Railroad cut through what is now Hamilton County, as did the Industrial. However, there was another development in these times that would ultimately become very important to the future restaurant business—the early stills were producing moonshine, and bootleggers were transporting it to innkeepers. Weary travelers could now have a bit of whiskey at the end of their journeys, and innkeepers began to see the benefit of having a space in their inns dedicated to selling it. Taverns were born. Around this time, coffee shops and drugstores were also selling food, and these were the earliest versions of restaurants as we know them today.

WARTIME RATIONING: THE EARLY 1900s

After the advent of railroads, automobiles were not far behind. Ford began producing the Model T (also known as the "Tin Lizzie," the "Leaping Lena" or the "flivver") in October 1908. The early twentieth century was a time of great prosperity, but just when the party was getting started, World War I came along. Food was heavily rationed, and folks ate at home, careful not to waste what might be needed for the war effort. America's allies in Europe were facing starvation as farmlands were transformed into battlefields. In 1918, shortly after the United States entered the war, President Woodrow Wilson established the U.S. Food Administration to manage wartime food conservation, distribution and transportation. Citizens were given rationing cards for foods that could be shipped overseas—specifically meat, wheat, butter and sugar. Drugstore counters and coffee shops adjusted their menus, offering "Meatless Tuesdays" and "Wheatless Wednesdays" in an effort to stay in business. Citizens focused their diets on perishables, fruits and vegetables that couldn't make the trip to Europe. World War I lasted from 1914 to 1918, but the rationing of meat, wheat, sugar and butter lasted much longer than that.

JAZZ, GIN AND CANAPÉS: THE EARLY 1920s

As the war ended and things slowly returned to normal on the home front, the evolution of the hospitality business came back to the forefront. The dawn of the Jazz Age brought about more nightlife, glitz and glamour. Speakeasies thrived, and the Roaring Twenties were in full swing. Coffee shops, drugstores and taverns evolved into speakeasies in an effort to compete, and people were certainly loving the idea of having a cocktail when they went out. But the focus was on music and alcohol; food was an afterthought, and most places simply served finger foods—"canapés," from the French—as a way to keep their inebriated patrons drinking. So, while food was served in these coffee shops–turned–clubs, they were just bite-sized things such as deviled eggs, finger sandwiches and shrimp cocktail. Good times were had by all. But every party has a pooper, and its name was Prohibition; although it didn't completely kill the party, it certainly made it more complicated.

PROHIBITION: THE PARTY'S ON HOLD (EVEN MORE SO IN INDIANA), 1920–1933

Prohibition, launched by the Volstead Act, was a nationwide ban on the production, importation, transportation and sale of alcoholic beverages. Note, however, that it didn't outlaw the *consumption* of alcoholic beverages. This meant that private ownership and consumption of alcohol in the home was still legal under federal law.

During Prohibition, the production, transportation and sale of alcoholic beverages certainly didn't stop—it just became illegal. This, of course, led to the rise of organized crime. Gangsters like Al Capone moved thousands of gallons of whiskey throughout the Midwest, and Indiana was no exception. Crime, in general, rose during this time. John Dillinger, Indiana's most notorious criminal, started with robbing grocery stores and saloons and eventually graduated to banks. It was a wild time of forces of extreme conservatism railing against extreme lawlessness, and those who were simply trying to make a buck serving food and drink to the general public were caught in the middle.

Prohibition also posed a huge public health risk, as unethical bootleggers, without risk of repercussions, produced "bathtub gin" (so named because the bottles were too big to fit in regular sinks). This alcohol, which often contained toxic substances such as antifreeze and embalming fluids, caused hundreds of thousands of imbibers to suffer vision loss, paralysis and sometimes even death.

Meanwhile, in Indiana, conservative forces behind the temperance movement had long beaten Prohibition to the punch. In 1855, they had managed to pass a pre-Prohibition law in Indiana, but it was struck down as unconstitutional three years later. They tried again in 1925 and managed to get the Wright "Bone Dry" law on the books. This meant that in addition to Prohibition laws, it was illegal in Indiana to possess any alcohol at all, even for medicinal purposes. At the time, alcohol, particularly whiskey and brandy, was widely prescribed by doctors—to adults and children alike—as a treatment for illnesses such as anemia, pneumonia and heart disease, and the alleged medicinal properties of alcohol were widely accepted.

But the Indiana chapter of the Anti-Saloon League, headquartered in Indianapolis, had other thoughts on that practice. The Woman's Christian Temperance Union and the Anti-Saloon League had been formed by women who believed that crime, gambling and domestic violence were a direct result of alcohol consumption, and they weren't about to make exceptions to the law—medicinal or otherwise. Drugstores and coffee shops that had adapted into speakeasies and saloons struggled to do business of any kind amidst the turmoil of both the hypervigilant temperance adherents and the gangsters. They simply could not win.

The "Noble Experiment" of Prohibition came to an end in 1933, mostly due to the fact that lawmakers realized enormous tax revenues were being lost because alcohol sales weren't being taxed. However, Indiana remains one of the last holdouts of some of the "blue laws" of that time. Although local brewpubs and wineries that have on-site production have been allowed to sell their products for carry-out on Sundays since 1971, Sunday sales for other retailers have only been allowed since 2018, and that change only happened after years of trying. Indiana is not alone in holding on to the temperance philosophies of the past—there are currently eleven other states that don't allow Sunday liquor sales.

THE GREAT DEPRESSION: 1929–1939

As if Prohibition wasn't challenging enough, struggling early restaurateurs would face yet another sobering event as the Great Depression descended on the country with the stock market crash of 1929. During the ten years of the Depression, restaurateurs were again forced, as they were during the war, to get creative with their menus and their marketing. So-called penny restaurants emerged; no menu item cost more than a dollar, coffee was a penny (with free refills, to boot) and restaurant owners attempted to lure customers away from their competitors with the first all-you-can-eat specials. Cooks were also forced to get creative; soups and stews took center stage, and animal parts that were once considered undesirable, such as knuckles and snouts, were brought to the center of the plate.

While one might have expected that life would have gotten easier for those trying to make a living in the restaurant business after Prohibition, things actually got a bit worse. In an effort to recoup lost bootlegging revenue, racketeers and gangsters began shaking down restaurants for a percentage of their paltry profits once they began legally serving alcohol. The "Sophie's Choice" restaurateurs had to make was to either pay the gangsters or pay those who offered protection from them.

THE WORLD WAR II EFFECT: IF IT'S FAST AND CHEAP, WE'LL EAT IT, LATE 1930s–MID-1940s

It would take another war to bring prosperity back to America and the next food revolution to the country. In the early 1940s, as the war efforts of World War II drew women out of the kitchen and into the workplace, convenience became the order of the day. In response to the perceived need for speed in sustenance, coffee shops and drugstore counters, long known as a place for lingering and exchanging news, gave way to drive-ins and diners focused on quick service. As industrial innovations began to automate food production, burger joints popped up on every corner, and a burger with fries could be had most anywhere for less than a dollar.

ED SULLIVAN, FORD: THE 1950s

In the 1950s, two suddenly pervasive things had a major impact on the American way of eating: televisions and cars. At the start of the decade, the population of the United States was just over 152 million. There were around 25 million registered vehicles, and just under 10 percent of U.S. households had a television set. By the end of the decade, there were 67 million cars registered, and a whopping 90 percent of households had a "boob tube." The first TV dinner hit the grocery frozen-food cases in the early 1950s. The age of convenience food had begun.

JAMES BEARD: A FOODIE AHEAD OF HIS TIME

James Beard was a pioneer in the foodie movement. *Photo by Bill Golladay.*

Long before the era of celebrity chefs would grip our collective consciousness, a gentleman named James Beard was railing against the utilitarian cuisine of the 1940s. Beard was born in Portland, Oregon, in 1903; his mother, Elizabeth, ran a boardinghouse, and the family spent summers at the beach fishing and gathering wild berries, so he learned the value of locally sourced ingredients at a very young age. After an unsuccessful attempt at a career in the theater, he turned to the food business and finally found his niche.

He released his first cookbook, *Hors d'Oeuvre and Canapés*, in 1940, and followed that with *Cook It Outdoors* in 1941. He would ultimately pen nearly thirty cookbooks, and he founded the James Beard Cooking School in 1955, with locations in New York City and Seaside, Oregon. He also hosted the first nationally televised cooking show in 1946. That effort turned out to be ill-fated, as less than 1 percent of American homes had television sets at the time, so his show did not enjoy the twenty-four-hours-a-day access that today's celebrity chefs do.

By the time he passed away in 1985, his name had become synonymous with the highest standards of American cuisine in both restaurant and home kitchens. Today, the foundation that bears his name annually bestows one of the culinary world's highest honors—the James Beard Awards. In previous years, Indiana chefs have been mostly left out of this party, as the foundation has seemed to mostly focus on high-profile restaurants on both coasts. However, that seems like it's about to change. Neal Brown has been a semifinalist twice, as has Indianapolis's Jonathan Brooks of Milktooth in Fountain Square. Steve Oakley of Indianapolis' Oakley's Bistro and Martha Hoover, owner of the Patachou organization, have recently been nominated as well.

The United States started to rely on filling meals that were simple to execute and prepared from prepackaged goods. These trends reflected a backlash from the rationing of the 1940s. There was also an influx of new cooking appliances to make the preparation of prepackaged food easier. Tuna casseroles and meatloaf ruled the day. However, the 1950s also brought an influx of exotic ethnic foods as the GIs returned from war.

As for television, it was not just a dinner guest; it was the guest of honor. Dinner hour revolved around whatever time folks' favorite shows came on. Mom was putting dinner on the table twice—once for the kids and again for her husband when he got home from work.

To feed the need to dine in front of the television, innovations such as TV trays emerged. These mobile dinner tables became the new place for families to gather at the end of the day. Even social gatherings centered around watching a show with the group. So-called TV cocktail parties emerged. The hostess would attempt to serve food that was easily eaten leaning over a TV tray, and party guests would dress up to huddle on a couch in a darkened living room to eat and take in the show. Society was glued to the tube.

Americans' devotion to their television schedule also gave rise to another dining trend: carry-out. As customers stayed home with their TV dinners, restaurants realized they had a problem. Leisurely dinners shared among families gathered at their favorite spots were becoming less frequent. To work around this trend and keep the doors open, savvy restaurant owners began to offer their fare packed up and ready to tote home to enjoy in front of the television. Pizza, chicken, hamburgers, Chinese food, Mexican food and barbecue were the most common carry-out meals, as they tended to travel and hold up better.

In addition to Americans' addiction to watching television, there was another, less innocuous reason for the surge in carry-out meals. During this era, African Americans were either not allowed into some restaurants or not allowed to sit in certain areas. Carry-out was sometimes the best or only option for them to purchase food from certain establishments. In many areas in the Midwest, this would not change until the 1970s or later.

During this time of massive population growth, suburban communities boomed. America became a society of car travel. So, when families did manage to pull themselves away from the television, piling the family into the car to drive somewhere just for the sake of driving became commonplace. As a result, drive-ins flourished, as did diners and fast-food joints where the family could all go together. As these establishments raced to outdo each other, trends such as waitresses on roller skates started to appear, as did food mascots and gimmicks.

FORGET JELL-O®, I ONLY EAT GOURMET: THE 1960s AND 1970s

In the late 1960s and early 1970s, a backlash to the automation and homogenization of food from the previous decade began. With even more women in the workforce and affluent women at home who had cooks and cleaning help, the oral tradition of passing down food and cooking knowledge from generation to generation seemed old-fashioned. Television began to play a role in how we learned to cook. New cooking shows started popping up on television, bringing food and techniques from foreign lands into homes in the Midwest without having to wait for a food trend to migrate from the coasts. Julia Child's show *The French Chef* ran from 1963 to 1973, and Graham Kerr's *The Galloping Gourmet* was on the air from 1969 to 1971. Both brought new techniques and food styles directly into homes in Hamilton County and across the United States, and the word "gourmet" entered our lexicon.

Child demonstrated dishes that most Americans had never heard of, such as boeuf bourguignon, quiche Lorraine, crêpes Suzette and bouillabaisse. While her recipes (as well as her stature) were daunting, her humorous, self-deprecating approach drew in viewers. When she made a mistake, she owned it and told her audience how to fix it. Kerr's show was a whimsical, fast-paced affair in which he dropped things, drank wine, spilled things, drank wine, burned things, drank more wine and ultimately leapt out of the kitchen and onto his couch and assured everyone that dinner would be just fine.

Across America, dinner parties were elevated to elegant, candlelit affairs, and gourmet restaurants started to pop up in larger metropolitan areas. Set against the uncertainty and unrest of the Vietnam War and the civil rights movement, food, which had always been a source of comfort, would also provide a sense of civility. Controlling and creating beauty on the plate became a way to feel in control of a seemingly out-of-control society.

These early TV chefs, the predecessors of today's Food Network stars, raised the bar a bit and inspired home cooks to up their game. More celebrity chefs, such as Paul Prudhomme and Emeril Lagasse, would soon follow in their footsteps.

THE FARM-TO-TABLE MOVEMENT IS BORN: MID-1970s

While mainstream America learned how to debone a chicken between commercials, restaurants in most parts of the country were still mainly focused on quick-serve—how they could feed the most people in the least amount of time. But a food revolution was brewing on the West Coast. Chefs railed against casual theme dining and looked to slow things down. It wasn't just the pace of the dining scene they were looking to change, though—it was also the quality. Chefs who looked to provide an extraordinary experience to their guests were tired of trying to put anemic, transit-weary and out-of-season produce on the plate. They began to make a conscious effort to use only ingredients that had been locally grown and developed relationships with farmers and other purveyors to grow or source exactly what they needed. What we now widely accept as the farm-to-table movement was born.

Year-round warm temperatures allowed West Coast chefs a luxury that chefs in other parts of the country didn't have; they could count on the fact that virtually any produce item they needed at any time of the year would be available from someone close by who was growing it. At the same time, the *nouvelle cuisine* movement was hitting France, a trend that moved from the heavy, sauce-based food of the "classique" French style to lighter, more delicate food with an increased emphasis on presentation.

Alice Waters is widely accepted to be the mother of the farm-to-table movement. She opened Chez Panisse in Berkeley, California, in 1971. Her French-inspired menu focused on using only the finest local ingredients and relied heavily on a network of supplies acquired through direct relationships with local ranchers, farmers and dairies.

CONSPICUOUS CONSUMERISM AND CELEBRITY CHEFS: THE 1980s

Despite the recession of the 1980s, Americans were dining out more than ever before. While dining out had previously been reserved for special occasions, it was now becoming more of a way of life. As cable television bloomed, more hours of broadcast time needed to be filled. The celebrity chef trend boomed, and those chefs opened upscale restaurants. Wolfgang Puck's Ma Maison opened in Los Angeles in 1982, and Emeril Lagasse's Commander's Palace followed in 1985.

The hallmark of the 1980s was over-the-top consumerism, and restaurants were no exception. While Madonna sang about being a "Material Girl," restaurants served supersized portions loaded with butter and rich, French-inspired sauces accompanied by à la carte side dishes and desserts big enough for a family of four to share. Steakhouses reigned supreme. Large-format bottles of wine appeared on wine lists, and steakhouses served gargantuan cuts of meat that only Fred Flintstone could have finished. Regular folks with normal appetites took the majority of their dinners home to the kids in elaborate foil-swan "doggy bags."

THE PENDULUM SETTLES IN THE CENTER, AND FARM-TO-TABLE COMES TO THE MIDWEST: THE 1990s TO TODAY

In the early 1990s, West Coast chefs had already pushed back against the massive portions and rich sauces of the '80s dining scene. Many of them were adopting a fusion style of cooking that integrated disparate cooking styles along with the continued commitment to fresh, locally sourced ingredients. This style of cooking came to be called California cuisine. In 1994, another legendary California restaurant was born as Thomas Keller opened the French Laundry in Yountville.

In 1990, the first farm-to-table restaurants started to appear in Chicago, and they sourced their ingredients from Illinois and Indiana farmers. The trend began to spread in the Midwest, but the term quickly became more of a marketing gimmick than a way of doing business. Restaurants would make the claim that they were "farm-to-table," but in reality, they may have been locally sourcing only one item, such as tomatoes. Consumers quickly caught on to this trick and began asking more questions of the servers as to the origins of the other meat and produce items on the menu. Today, many restaurants are listing their local vendors on the menu to convey their commitment to sourcing their menu items locally.

Over the years, restaurants have adapted to the times as the pendulum of dining trends has swung wildly from one extreme to another. Restaurants have competed to be the cheapest or the most expensive. They've attempted to set themselves apart with gimmicks and kitsch. They've served rich sauces and decadent desserts one year and bare bones, minimalist food that left diners feeling starved but sophisticated the next. They're nothing if not resourceful.

Today, the pendulum has settled somewhere in the middle in central Indiana and across the country. Chefs will certainly still try to find ways to set themselves apart by combining ingredients in previously unimagined ways (think roasted garlic ice cream or peanut butter–topped hamburgers) or innovative food techniques (like molecular gastronomy). But we're in a pretty good place right now. We have a wonderful mélange of dining options that represent the way we live today. One of the best trends of recent years is that of casual but upscale restaurants that welcome families but don't condescend to young diners. Junior foodies are no longer always relegated to choosing between chicken fingers with applesauce or cheese quesadillas. They can often now opt for smaller portions of what their parents are enjoying, whether it's a lovely piece of grilled salmon or petite filet.

Diners in Hamilton County and beyond can choose made-from-scratch meals to take home; sit down to a beautifully presented meal replete with white tablecloths, fresh flowers and candles; or enjoy an artisan, thin-crust pizza with locally sourced toppings. Hopefully, those same diners are choosing to support local, chef- and owner-operated establishments that also choose to support local growers, farmers and purveyors. The end result of that beautiful symmetry is stronger local economies and communities that engage with each other and thrive.

Sadly, many restaurants of the past have come and gone without much fanfare. Photographs of the food, owners or patrons are hard to come by. This is in sharp contrast to today's era of social media, in which few meals go undocumented. Restaurant selfies and food posts crowd the internet, and servers probably need to add "photographer" to their job descriptions. This is not a bad thing. Restaurants and the food they serve have been an integral part of the fabric of our culture for hundreds of years, but they've rarely gotten the attention they deserve.

Much like the coffee shops, drugstores and diners of yesteryear, restaurants of today—more than ever—are the places we go to celebrate, commiserate and engage with others and sustain both our bodies and our souls.

2

CONNERS, QUAKERS AND CORN PONE

A Brief Look at the History of Hamilton County

Mention Hamilton County cuisine—or Indiana food in general—to foodies outside of the state, and they might snidely reply, "Is there anything other than corn?" Fair enough. Indiana has long been known for this culinary icon, and Hamilton County has been no exception. Well before the upscale housing developments, storefronts, theaters, parks and malls that fill Hamilton County today, ambling country roads cut a patchwork through rolling fields of soybeans, wheat, grain, cows and, of course, the ubiquitous corn.

In fact, Indiana's love affair with corn is documented as early as 1830, when a gentleman named George Shirts ran the first hotel and erected the first known frame house in Hamilton County. This house was later turned into a tavern in Noblesville. George's wife, Rebecca, made what was apparently a to-die-for corn pone, which was a very simple and popular dish reminiscent of a corn pancake. Rebecca's dish was so popular that Robert Stitt, a Noblesville resident, was stopped one day on his way home by a stranger from out of town on horseback. The stranger said to him, "My friend, can you tell me where I can find the woman who makes the good corn pone?" Stitt replied, "Well, if it's the woman that stays at the tavern that you are after, you're on the right track. Keep straight ahead until you come to the sign board."

So, even in the days before Yelp, TripAdvisor and local dining guides were at our fingertips on our mobile devices, travelers were looking for the best food and drink the area had to offer—even if it meant riding their horses a little off the beaten path.

THE BIRTH OF THE COUNTY: THE EARLY 1800s

It's nearly impossible to travel through Hamilton County without coming across the name Conner. You'll find streets, shopping complexes, housing subdivisions and creeks bearing the name—and for good reason. Hamilton County wouldn't be here today without William Conner, the first settler in Hamilton County. He arrived in 1800 with his older brother John. William married a woman named Mekinges from the Delaware Indian tribe in 1802 and would ultimately serve as an interpreter at the signing of the Treaty of St. Mary's in 1818, where his father-in-law, Chief William Anderson, gave possession of the Delaware Indians' land to the U.S. government.

By 1822, Conner realized there were enough settlers in the area to apply to the Indiana legislature for a charter to become an independent county under Indiana law. The application was passed and approved in January 1823, and Hamilton County (named for Alexander Hamilton) became the twenty-ninth county in Indiana. Naturally, William Conner's house served as the county circuit court.

Conner would ultimately send his wife and their six children west but remain in Indiana himself. He then married seventeen-year-old Elizabeth Chapman, and they went on to have ten more children.

In 1830, the first census of the county showed a population of 1,757 with Noblesville as the county seat. Over the next decade, the population grew as Scotch-Irish, Irish Catholics, Germans and Quakers started to arrive. Things were going pretty well until the national depression of 1837 hit. Banks failed, the state was essentially bankrupt and immigration slowed. Still, by 1840, the population had grown to 9,855.

In the 1840s, Eagletown, Arcadia and Clarksville were established. In 1851, the game changed considerably as the first railroad reached Noblesville and brought with it new immigrants, many of them refugees from Europe. By the 1860s, the population of Hamilton County had doubled again. The Civil War had a dramatic impact on Hamilton County as men joined the Indiana infantry and the Quakers, who opposed slavery, became actively involved in the Underground Railroad. By the time the Civil War ended, Hamilton County had lost nearly 300 souls.

The 1860s saw the creation of Sheridan as well as the first women's suffrage group meeting. Fishers came along in the 1870s. The 1880 census showed nearly 25,000 folks living in Hamilton County, and the first phone company was formed.

THE GREAT SQUIRREL STAMPEDE OF 1826

This astonishing phenomenon was not unique to Hamilton County, as the massive wave of squirrels started somewhere west of Hamilton County and ate their way east. But in a book called *A History of the Formation, Settlement and Development of Hamilton County, Indiana, From the Year 1818 to the Close of the Civil War*, Noblesville lawyer Augustus F. Shirts wrote about the devastating effect that the squirrel migration had on local farmers.

"The squirrels passed through from west to east," he wrote. "Their numbers could not be estimated. The time occupied in passing was about two weeks. They destroyed all the corn in the fields they passed over. They could not be turned in their course, but went straight on in the route taken. When they came to the White River, they entered the water at once and swam across."

Naturalists have theorized that the squirrel stampede was triggered by the fact that so much forest was cleared in a short period of time, which disrupted the squirrels' natural habitat and caused a food shortage for the creatures.

NATURAL GAS BOOMS AND COMMERCE: THE LATE 1800s

The late 1800s were a booming time in Hamilton County. Natural gas was discovered here in 1887. As was true in many other parts of the state, the boom brought great growth in commerce in the forms of mills and factories and newly paved streets. The county also received national attention when Benjamin Harrison was elected president in 1888. Our twenty-third president was a U.S. senator from Indiana and the grandson of William Henry Harrison. He had friends in Sheridan and frequently visited for hunting trips. In 1891, the first electric company was organized in Noblesville, and in 1895, the Wild Opera House was built.

By 1900, the county's population was nearly 30,000. However, a bust was on the horizon as the once bountiful natural gas supply began to fail. In an effort to circumvent the short supply, the first hydroelectric dams were built. There was still slow but steady progress—the railroads continued to thrive, the interurban lines made their way through Hamilton County and libraries were built.

AXES AND ALCOHOL, WHITE CAPPERS AND WILD WOMEN: THE LATE 1800s

Indiana had a pretty big head start on Prohibition with the temperance movement, which enjoyed strong support across Hamilton County. However, alcohol wasn't the only thing moral folks had to worry about, as another form of commerce had developed on the "wrong" side of the tracks, particularly in Noblesville—prostitution.

In 1883, a Hamilton County newspaper called the *Republican-Ledger* ran an exposé, entitled "Noblesville's Bagnios," about Noblesville's "houses of assignation." The articles claimed that there were twenty-six such houses in Noblesville and detailed not just the locations of the houses but also the names of its alleged employees, including Jenny Adams (a.k.a. the "Iron Sheet Blonde") and Bell Hooper (a.k.a. the "Drum Major").

The articles began after a mob burned down an alleged house of ill repute on the south side of town. This type of vigilante behavior would become widespread as citizens took the enforcement of morality into their own hands not just with houses of ill repute, but also with any business that served alcohol. In Westfield, saloon owners slept with one eye open as axe-wielding women demonstrated their disapproval by smashing storefronts and destroying businesses. The situation became even worse as the Ku Klux Klan and the White Cappers joined forces with the more passive teetotalers.

DEPRESSION, WAR, FIRE AND FLOOD: DARK TIMES IN THE EARLY 1900s

As was true across the country, times were fairly dark in Hamilton County throughout the first half of the twentieth century. In addition to two world wars and the Great Depression, several tragedies would also strike—a massive flood that hit the state in 1913 wrought severe damage across the county, and fires in Sheridan, Carmel and Cicero brought great losses as well. In fact, chunks of Hamilton County history have been forever lost due to records in government offices being destroyed in these disasters.

The census of 1920 showed the first downturn in the county's population, to 24,222, as a result of the gas bust and the trend of folks moving from rural areas to urban centers.

THE 1960s TO TODAY

By 1960, the population was 40,132, and highways began to connect the county. In 1965, another tragedy—the Palm Sunday tornadoes—resulted in 138 deaths statewide, with 6 of them occurring in Hamilton County.

The 1970s saw the opening of reservoirs and state parks, which led to more recreation and housing, and as the temperance movement loosened its grip on the county, Westfield finally had a tavern that operated without fear of getting axed. By 1980, the population had doubled again from its 1960s numbers to just over 82,000. Hamilton County had voted in two female mayors; Patricia Logan served as Noblesville's mayor from 1980 to 1988, and Jane Reiman served as Carmel's mayor for two terms, as well, from 1980 to 1987.

There was also a reversal of the earlier trend of folks choosing to move into urban centers. As cities became overcrowded and expensive, families were choosing newer homes with larger lots, and the suburbs of Indianapolis, along with many other cities across the United States, saw population booms. By 2000, the population of Hamilton County was 187,740; in 2010, it was 274,569. As of 2018, it was at nearly 350,000, making Hamilton County both the fastest-growing and most affluent county in Indiana.

Hamilton County is currently made up of nine townships: Adams, Jackson, White River, Washington, Noblesville, Wayne, Clay, Delaware and Fall Creek. Each of these townships contains a mix of variously sized cities and towns, as well as over 150 unincorporated towns. Noblesville remains the county seat.

NOBLESVILLE

The Conner family settled the land upon which Noblesville currently sits in the early 1800s and established the first trading post. In 1823, William Conner, along with Josiah Polk, laid out what is now Noblesville's downtown. In 1824, Noblesville would be designated the Hamilton County seat, and it was incorporated in 1851.

One popular legend claims that Noblesville is named for Lavinia Noble, to whom Josiah Polk was engaged. In a precursor to the dramatic marriage proposals and prom invitations of today, Polk not only built a house for Lavinia but also placed a vegetable garden spelling out her name in front of the house and asked the town's forefathers to name the town after her. Lavinia was apparently mortified by this show of affection and refused the proposal.

Locals might tell you that the name came from another woman whom Josiah Polk allegedly courted, Catherine Noble (the daughter of Indiana

Downtown Noblesville, circa 1900. *Courtesy of Hamilton East Public Library, Joe Roberts Collection.*

Couden's Bakery in Noblesville, circa 1900. *Courtesy of Hamilton East Public Library, Joe Roberts Collection.*

The Soda Inn in Noblesville, circa 1900. *Courtesy of Hamilton East Public Library, Joe Roberts Collection.*

governor Noah Noble). The hole in this theory is that Catherine would only have been one year old when Noblesville was formed. The real truth behind the name will probably never be known.

In the mid-to-late 1800s, railroads were completed and natural gas was discovered in the area. These events led to a population and building boom. The centerpieces of Noblesville's downtown square, the Hamilton County Courthouse and the Hamilton County Sheriff's Residence (now home to the Hamilton County Historical Society) were built between 1876 and 1879. Flour mills were a thriving business in the early 1900s. Noblesville's famous Model Mill is now home to a multiuse office and event space called the Mill Top.

As the population grew and diversified in the early 1900s, race relations were certainly an issue. The Ku Klux Klan was active in Noblesville at the time, and one of the most notorious trials to ever take place in the Hamilton County Courthouse was the trial of D.C. Stephenson, a former Grand Dragon. When Stephenson was ultimately convicted of second-degree murder in the death of Madge Oberholtzer, the Klan's influence began to fade. The Hamilton County jail housed another famous prisoner in 1950, when Charles Manson did some time there as a teenager for auto theft.

FISHERS

Conner also settled what is now Fishers, and the town was platted by Salathial Fishers, for whom it was named. In 1849, the Peru and Indianapolis Railroad, which took travelers from Indianapolis to Chicago, was built. Fishers Station (or Fishers Switch), as it was then called, was one of the first stops. In 1908, the name was shortened to Fishers. In 1934, Eli Lilly, the founder of Eli Lilly and Company (currently one of the largest employers in Indiana), purchased the Conner Farm and had it restored with the help of Earlham College. Both the trading post and the log cabin that William Conner built on his land in the Fishers area are preserved and open for touring at the Conner Prairie living history museum on Allisonville Road.

Fishers is one of the fastest-growing communities in Indiana. In 1960, the census reported a mere 344 inhabitants, and Fishers was still just a stop on the way from Indianapolis to parts north. But the population continued to grow, and on January 1, 2015, Fishers transitioned from

Downtown Fishers in 1977. *Courtesy of the City of Fishers.*

a town to a city and elected Scott Fadness as its first mayor. The city of Fishers now boasts a population of just over 90,000 along with the first IKEA in the state of Indiana. New businesses and developments are blossoming every day.

WESTFIELD

Founded in 1834, Westfield followed closely on the heels of Noblesville, but the character of Westfield was much different, as it was founded by Quakers Asa Bales, Ambrose Osborne and Simon Moon. Many believe Westfield was developed as a stop on the Underground Railroad, which helped slaves escape to Canada. The name Westfield comes from the Westfield Friends Monthly Meeting, which was conducted by a group of antislavery Quakers from North Carolina. Westfield was incorporated as a town in 1848. While saloons and taverns were thriving in neighboring

Westfield's Main Street, circa 1960. *Courtesy of the Westfield Washington Historical Society and Museum.*

Noblesville, the scene was much different in Westfield. It was a dry town and remained so until the 1970s.

On January 1, 2008, Westfield was incorporated as a city and elected its first mayor, Andy Cook. The population dramatically grew with the annexation of Washington Township to the south. The 2015 census reported a population of 36,854—nearly four times the population in 2000.

CARMEL

Carmel was settled by Quakers and was originally platted in 1837 under the name Bethlehem. The first general store was constructed in 1837, and a post office was built in 1846. The post office caused some unanticipated trouble for Bethlehem, as there was already a town in Indiana with the same name. As a result, in 1874, a referendum vote was taken, and the town was officially incorporated and renamed Carmel.

The Monon Railroad rails, laid in 1882, brought about a rapid expansion of the population, and Carmel has seen continuous growth ever since. Under the auspices of six-term mayor Jim Brainard, Carmel has experienced a massive boom in population, development and enterprise. Carmel now boasts the world-class Center for the Performing Arts, a campus of three separate performance spaces: the Palladium, a 1,600-seat concert hall; the Tarkington, a 500-seat proscenium theater; and the Studio, an intimate, 200-seat black box theater.

The newly developed Midtown area joins the Arts and Design District on Main Street with the City Centre to the south, where the Center for Performing Arts is housed. Midtown will eventually feature a center green and numerous mixed-use buildings that will house restaurants, apartments and offices.

Carmel's West Main Street, circa 1920. *Courtesy of the Carmel Clay Historical Society.*

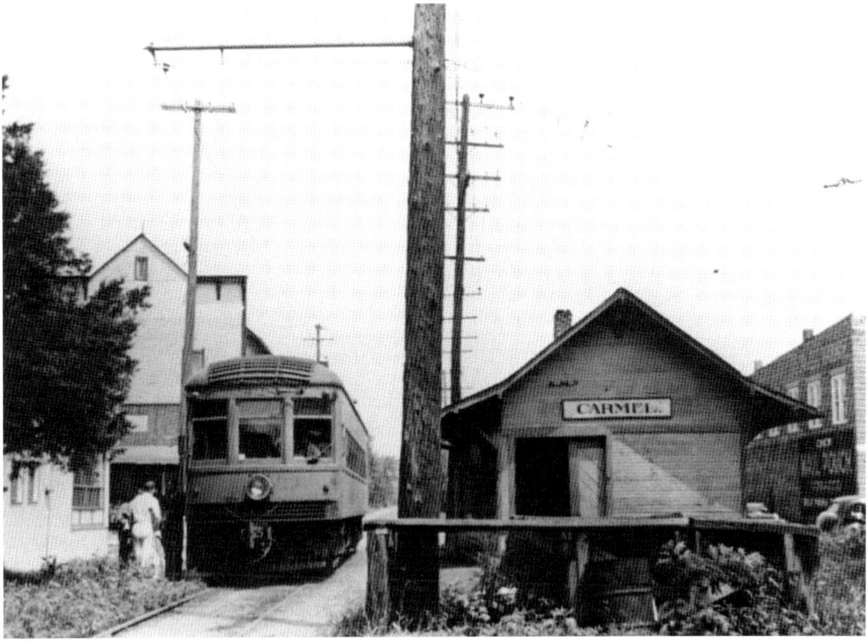

The Carmel stop on the Interurban Railroad, circa 1890. *Courtesy of Hamilton East Public Library, Joe Roberts Collection.*

Carmel also boasts over one hundred roundabouts—more than any city in the United States. This is ironic, given the fact that one of the first stop-and-go traffic signals in the country was invented and installed at the intersection of Main Street and Range Line Road in 1924 by a gentleman named Leslie Haines. At that time, the population of Carmel was less than 400; currently, Carmel's population is well over 90,000.

ATLANTA

In 1834, General Michael Sheil and his wife, Bridget, settled in the area that would become Atlanta. Sheil built a trading post in 1836 to trade with the Miami Indians and named the area Sheilville. In 1835, another settler named Caleb Sparger built a trading post nearby and called it Spargersville. In 1846, Andrew Tucker bought some land from Sheil and laid out a town he called Buena Vista. The arrival of the Indianapolis, Peru & Chicago Railway in Buena Vista caused it to thrive, while Sheilville declined.

Buena Vista would soon be forced to change its name, though, as it was also discovered that this name was taken by a town that already had a post office. In 1885, the town was renamed Atlanta, most probably influenced by men returning home from the Civil War. Atlanta was incorporated in 1900, and the discovery of natural gas soon brought about a boom in the population. Businesses flourished, including six saloons, bakeries, groceries, hotels and a bank. In the heyday of the gas boom, there were ten to twelve active natural gas wells, and they brought great prosperity to Atlanta. But in the 1930s, the gas pocket went dry, and Atlanta suffered a gradual decline. The current population hovers around 700—less than half its number of inhabitants during the gas boom.

CICERO

Cicero was founded in 1835, taking its name from the nearby Cicero Creek. The post office was founded in 1839. The arrival of the first railroad (in 1853) brought about a growth in industry, and Cicero also experienced a gas boom. The first bridge in Hamilton County was built in Cicero in 1838. In 1870, that original bridge was converted into a covered bridge and painted red. The Red Bridge became the town's most famous landmark, but in 1950, the bridge was torn down to make way for Morse Reservoir. The reservoir has brought about a lakeside lifestyle, and Cicero offers the charm of a small town with the convenience of being near a big city. Today, Cicero is considered Hamilton County's finest recreational and resort community with a population of nearly 5,000 people.

SHERIDAN

Sheridan was once the second-largest town in Hamilton County. Originally named Millwood, its origins are difficult to pinpoint due to a disastrous fire in 1913 that destroyed the town hall and all the records within. It is known, though, that Egbert Higbee acquired land in the area that had been previously owned by George Boxley. He laid out a town called Millwood and filed a town plat in April 1866. Another Boxley—a gentleman named Caswell—laid out a plat adjoining Higbee's and also named it Millwood. An application for Millwood's post office was submitted in January 1871. In a now-common occurrence, it was discovered that there was already a village in Indiana named Millwood. The town's name was changed to Sheridan in honor of the Union general Philip Sheridan.

In 1882, with the arrival of the Monon Railroad, Sheridan experienced a commercial and population boom that led to its incorporation in 1886. In the late 1800s and early 1900s, Sheridan experienced another boom with the discovery of natural gas. The natural gas supply quickly ran out, but during this period of prosperity, many buildings were erected, and a downtown emerged. With the fire of 1913 and the bust of the gas market, Sheridan's growth leveled out, and today, the population remains around 3,000.

STRAWTOWN

Strawtown is currently an unincorporated town in White River Township. The 2016 census did not count the population of Strawtown, specifically, but the population within a five-mile radius of the center is 6,479. Strawtown was once an Indian village. It was laid out in 1819 by Bicknell Cole and William Conner and is significant because it was the halfway point between Anderson and Indianapolis. It was possibly named after a Delaware Indian chief named Straw or Strawbridge. It was settled by Delaware Indians following the 1795 treaty in which the Miami and Shawnee tribes offered them land in the White River Basin. Due to the fact that the nearest railroad was four miles to the west, Strawtown never enjoyed the population growth that many other Hamilton County communities did.

IN SUMMARY

Hamilton County, like most counties in Indiana, grew from humble beginnings. Some communities thrived, while others perished. With interesting inventions, terrible tragedies, pioneering entrepreneurs and growing pains, Hamilton County slowly began to evolve. Through it all, folks gathered in whatever form of a restaurant was available to them—whether it was a coffee shop, soda fountain, diner or steakhouse. Any trip down memory lane with a longtime Hamilton County resident will inevitably involve the mention of a restaurant from days gone by that still holds a special place in their hearts—a place where they celebrated birthdays, holidays and good report cards, hung out with their friends, went on their first date, held wedding rehearsals and then celebrated anniversaries. The owners and employees at these restaurants are also a part of the fabric of those memories. They helped plan surprise parties, funeral lunches, wedding proposals and retirement dinners. They watched children grow up and become regular customers, bringing their own children into the restaurant and teaching them table manners.

This book is about the family-owned establishments of both yesterday and today. It does not include chain restaurants unless the chain was a franchise owned by a Hamilton County resident and had a significant impact on the local restaurant scene. We will first look at the restaurants in these cities and towns that are fondly remembered but no longer exist.

These early restaurants obviously did not focus on haute cuisine. They were owned by folks trying to make a living by providing quick and inexpensive sustenance to locals and travelers. Many of their menus were quite similar to their competitors', so the challenge was in finding a convenient location; making sure prices were competitive; and being open for breakfast, lunch and dinner to capture all the revenue they possibly could. These hospitality pioneers paved the way for the independently owned restaurants of today, and for that, they're not only notable, they're invaluable.

3

HAMILTON COUNTY FOOD OF THE PAST

NOBLESVILLE

Noblesville has the longest history of all the cities and towns in Hamilton County. As a result, it also has more historic buildings and restaurants than the rest of the county. Longtime Noblesville residents have memories of so many different eateries from their childhoods, each unique in its own way. Vestiges of many of them remain today. Some of the buildings still stand, housing a new restaurant or a different enterprise altogether. Fair warning—several of these eateries and gathering spots have a bit of a checkered past, so, reader beware!

Aunt Bee's Chicken

Driving down Tenth Street, you'll see the Hamilton Hill Animal Hospital. No, the giant white rooster statue in front of it does not indicate that the veterinary practice specializes in treating farm animals. The rooster is the last vestige of Aunt Bee's Chicken, a restaurant that saw its heyday from 1969 to 1992. Serving some of the best broasted chicken in the area, Charlie and Susan Meredith named their restaurant in honor of the kindly Aunt Bee from *The Andy Griffith Show*, who was always in the kitchen and feeding the people she loved.

The rooster was not a part of the original décor plan. The Merediths received the giant fiberglass fowl as a free gift with purchase when they bought some extra frying equipment. Little did they know that the gift would be ten feet tall and made of four hundred pounds of fiberglass. Defying the laws of physics, they originally managed to "roost" the bird on the roof of the building, but additions, improvements and building codes eventually

Opposite: Wild's Opera House in Noblesville, the first opera house in Hamilton County, late 1800s. *Courtesy of Hamilton East Public Library, Joe Roberts Collection.*

Right: The Grand Hotel in Noblesville, late 1800s. *Courtesy of Hamilton East Public Library, Joe Roberts Collection.*

Below: The giant rooster from Aunt Bee's restaurant still stands today. *Photo by author.*

required them to move it to the parking lot in front of the building, where it still proudly stands today. The current owner of the building just didn't feel it was right to take it down. It's been a part of the Noblesville landscape for many years.

Beanie's Cafeteria

Beanie's Cafeteria opened its doors in 1902 at 173 North Ninth Street. Paul ("Beanie Sr.") and Marcellus ("Beanie Jr.") Paskins ran it in turn until 1969, when they sold it to Horst Langner, who ran it until 1991. The restaurant weathered many storms, including food rationing during World War II, when people lined up around the block to get in. It was sold again and finally closed its doors in 1991 after a nearly ninety-year run.

Blue Ribbon Dairy Drive-In

The Blue Ribbon Dairy Drive-In was a popular hangout for families and date-night spot for teenagers in the 1950s. Interestingly, though, it was never intended to sell ice cream. It was founded as a dairy by Riley Sanders, Russell Moore and Dr. Ray Shanks. In 1939, they built a milk-bottling plant, and in 1942, Wayne Moser joined the business, which boomed, and Moser ran it for thirty years. Progress came along in the form of cardboard milk cartons, and the process of trying to switch the facility to packaging milk in cartons instead of bottles was not feasible for them. So, in 1952, they sold their milk-bottling and delivery services to Maplehurst and started selling ice cream. The ice cream shop eventually blossomed into a full-fledged drive-in that served grilled sandwiches, French fries and pizza. In 1973, the Blue Ribbon closed after Moser, who had run it for thirty-one years, passed away.

Noblesville native and artist Rodney Reveal has captured many of Noblesville's historic restaurants on canvas. He believes that he has also captured precious moments in residents' lives in the process.

"You know, without these places when we were young, I don't know how any of us would have found spouses!" Reveal muses. "They were the social center of town. It was where you went when something good happened and the place you went when you needed company. People look at my paintings and say, 'Oh, I met my husband there!' or 'I got engaged there!' It was how people connected."

Burger Chef

The Burger Chef was located at the intersection of South Tenth and Pleasant Streets. The chain was founded in Indianapolis in 1954 and eventually expanded to over two thousand locations across the United States. Burger Chef's original hamburger sold for fifteen cents. Burger Chef is credited as having created the first combination meal offering with its "Value Combo" of a burger, fries and a soft drink for forty-five cents. Burger Chef also created a "Fun Meal" for kids in the early 1970s. The company unsuccessfully sued when McDonald's launched a very similar concept called "Happy Meals" in 1979. In 1982, the Burger Chef chain was sold to the parent company of Hardee's, and all the existing restaurants were converted to the Hardee's brand.

Clancy's

The original Clancy's was opened by Carl Fogelsong at Tenth and Maple Streets in downtown Noblesville. Clancy's was one of the first "double drive-through" restaurants in the area. The central tenets of Clancy's philosophy were "quality, value and cleanliness." It seems like a pretty straightforward concept, but it appeared to be a breakthrough at the time. The simple menu and excellent products were widely applauded, and customers clamored to get in the door. Due to this success, a second Clancy's location opened in Noblesville on State Road 32.

In 1966, Carl's brother Gale joined the team, and they expanded into Ohio. With every successful opening, the brothers' business ambition continued to grow. They expanded into other cities and towns in Indiana as well as Ohio, Kentucky and Tennessee.

By the late 1960s and mid-1970s, there were a total of thirty Clancy's restaurants. Their growth seemed unstoppable until Goliath came to the Midwest in the mid-1970s and started gobbling up their burger-and-fries–loving customers. That Goliath's name was McDonald's. As McDonald's staked its claim in the territory, Burger King and Wendy's were not far behind. This led to loss of market share for our hometown heroes.

In an effort to regroup, Clancy's took a stab at a high-end restaurant and catering facility. It failed. They attributed the failure to the fact that they were minority partners in the business and weren't allowed to make changes as they saw fit. But in 1981, Carl's son Perry, armed with a degree from the

The original Clancy's logo featuring the friendly cop. *Photo provided.*

Kelly School of Business at Indiana University, helped turn things around. They found a closed property and turned it into a casual theme dining experience. This was the new wave of dining in Indiana, and it was broadly appealing—not too fancy, but a place where a family could sit down and enjoy something for everyone (along with the all-important cocktail).

The new concept was called Grindstone Charley's. The first restaurant was in Noblesville. As it gained popularity, Clancy's began to expand again. By 1996, there were thirteen locations, and sales were booming. Unfortunately, in the mid-1990s, history repeated itself as other national casual theme chains such as Applebee's, Texas Roadhouse and O'Charley's started to encroach on smaller local businesses. Carl passed away in 2006, but Perry's son Blake joined the business in 2010, and Clancy's, Incorporated, began clawing back its share of the market. With four Grindstone Charley's locations and one Clancy's remaining in Sydney, Ohio, the business continues to look for new opportunities for expansion. They have opened a new concept called Michaelangelo's Italian Bistro in the spot where Clancy's drive-through once thrived on State Road 32. They are also currently considering a new concept near the spot where it all began in downtown Noblesville, as the original Noblesville Clancy's was demolished in February 2005 to make room for a parking lot for the new city hall.

Classic Kitchen

In 1980, as steakhouses (both chains and locally owned places) were cornering the market in the central Indiana dining scene, a few local chefs started to push back. It seemed to them that not every meal needed to consist of a steak, a baked potato loaded with sour cream and a sorry attempt at fresh vegetables with a sprig of parsley for color.

In Noblesville, that chef was Steve Keneipp. The Classic Kitchen took a *nouvelle cuisine* approach to dining that resulted in either gushing fans or folks grumbling that they'd just emptied their wallets and left hungry.

One such gushing fan was Susan Guyett, then a food writer at the *Indianapolis Star*, who gave the Classic Kitchen a four-star rating but warned, "Meat and potato types should look elsewhere. You won't find a steak anywhere on the menu."

What diners did find on the menu were elaborate dishes such as the "Chicken Grande Hotel Olaffson," a breadcrumb-and-coconut-encrusted chicken breast served with steamed and raw vegetables and the signature red beans and rice, as well as champagne-poached salmon, Veal Florentine and English chicken liver paté. Meals started with a generous basket of hearty, freshly baked herb bread. Desserts were adventurous, as well, even by today's standards, with black pepper ice cream and twenty-three-karat-gold–topped saffron ice cream among the choices.

Given that the restaurant had only forty-two seats, service was intimate, with the chef/owner himself describing the menu choices to each table in lieu of a menu. Keneipp closed Classic Kitchen in 2007 to pursue other interests and sold the building to Tanya Marshall, who owns Heavenly Sweets.

Fryberger's Tea Room

In the 1930s and early 1940s, folks flocked from all over to eat fried chicken and corn fritters at Fryberger's Tea Room. Originally located on the northeast corner of Tenth Street and Maple Avenue and later moved to South Ninth Street, it was run by a mother-daughter team. The daughter, Pauline Fryberger, is said to have run the dining room with an iron fist. The servers there, all young ladies, were known as "Polly's Girls," and as part of their training, they were taken downtown to the LS Ayres Tea Room to observe proper tearoom service.

The tearoom was modeled after European-style salons and featured crisp white linens, fine china and fresh flowers on the tables. It was a popular spot for ladies' clubs to meet.

Lagoon Lodge

Perhaps the most notorious of all the historic places in or around Noblesville is the Lagoon Lodge. According to a 1978 article in the *Hamiltonian Magazine*, the lodge was built in 1923 as a family resort by two brothers who were executives with the Midwest Railroad and planned for it to be a family retreat. Much of the building was made from dismantled boxcars. However, the brothers went bankrupt shortly after the lodge was finished. The lodge then changed hands a few times and was eventually acquired by a former sheriff who, by most accounts, ran it as a dance hall. Although there is little documentation to support the accounts, most locals grew up learning the story that John Dillinger and Al Capone and their gangs spent quite a bit of time at the lodge enjoying mint juleps on the veranda.

There's also evidence to support the fact that there was more than illegal drinking going on at the lodge. The nine small bedrooms down the long upstairs hallway are said to have been used as a house of ill repute, and some of the rooms even feature a secret compartment cut into the floor—perfect for hiding weapons and bottles of bootleg whiskey. It's also said that Aunt Belle, the proprietress of the establishment, kept a raft moored in the lagoon and loaded her still on it anytime there was a raid. She would push the still out into the middle of the lagoon until the raid was over, then reel it back in when the coast was clear.

The Lagoon Lodge closed in 1933. It's now home to the Riverbend Campground, and while good times are certainly still had here, things have settled down quite a bit.

Louie's Bakery

According to Noblesville native Danny Weaver, Louie's Bakery was located in the space that now houses Vintage Guitars (look for the white building with a guitar mounted on top; it's just across the street from the giant rooster). According to Weaver, pastries weren't the only source of revenue at Louie's. Weaver recalls that it was common knowledge back in the day that there was a secret brothel in the basement. If you were in the market for something other than a doughnut, you simply went to the counter and ordered a "chocolate éclair," and you would be ushered downstairs.

Lutz's Steakhouse

Dave and Nancy Lutz were fixtures on the Noblesville dining scene for nearly thirty years. The Lutzes bought the restaurant (located at 3100 Westfield Road and previously called Calloway's Steakhouse) in 1983 after having had only one meal there. They worked on creating an ambiance similar to the atmosphere in the bar on the television series *Cheers*—all comers were treated like regulars, and everyone knew your name and your family. Noblesville's landscape was very different then. In sharp contrast to today, Lutz's was one of only about ten sit-down restaurants in town, and deer regularly roamed near the parking lot.

A classic supper club of the time, Lutz's Steakhouse featured live music along with their steaks, baked potatoes and seafood. They were also known for signature items such as homemade butterscotch rolls and French-fried lobster.

When Dave passed away in 2009, Nancy continued to run the restaurant until she finally decided to close the doors and retire in 2014, when she was seventy-two. In the restaurant's later years of operation, chef Sherry King, in an early farm-to-table effort, created a garden outside of the restaurant in which she grew tomatoes, peppers, cabbage, onions and fresh herbs.

Ramsey's Drive-In

Visitors who park their cars at today's entrance to Noblesville's Forest Park would have no idea of the good times that took place for many years on that very spot. What is now a parking lot was originally the site of Ramsey's Drive-In (and, prior to that, White's Drive-in). It was a swinging hangout especially popular with teens in the 1950s and '60s, and one of the best stops when they were out cruising. Garland and Edna Ramsey operated the drive-in for ten years, even adding a canopy and carhops for curbside service. The proximity to the park and the river was a major draw but also ultimately led to the business's downfall, as the site was prone to frequent flooding. Ramsey's closed in the late 1960s, and the building was razed in the early 1970s.

The 500 Bar

Along with Louie's Bakery, Noblesville native Danny Weaver recalled the 500 Bar on South Eighth Street, which he likened to a haunt of "Bad, Bad Leroy Brown."

"Seemed like there was a stabbing there every twenty minutes," said Weaver. "You didn't go in there unless you were looking for trouble." According to Weaver, there was also a brothel upstairs at the 500 Bar and a secret code to get up there. (The code, which remains a secret, undoubtedly had nothing to do with pastries.)

The 500 Bar, which featured a honky-tonk-style sing-along, billed itself as the "Gayest Spot in Town." Lyric sheets for the sing-along included such songs as: "A Shanty in Old Shanty Town," "The Drunkard Song" and "If You Knew Susie Like I Knew Susie" (including the classic lyrics, "There's none so classy as this fair lassie/Oh, oh, holy Moses what a chassis").

However, both the trouble and the gaiety came to an end in February 1977. The building had recently been purchased by new owners, who

Firefighters work to put out the 500 Bar fire in 1977. *Courtesy of the Hamilton County Historical Society.*

were having some remodeling done. During regular business hours, the remodelers worked on a weight-bearing wall that caused the entire second floor of the building to fall into the first. The incident killed fifty-eight-year-old William Harris (who was the father of one of Weaver's friends) and injured nine others, including Harris's son Michael. To compound matters, a fire ensued, and the building quickly burned down. No remnants of the building remain today.

The Hamilton Restaurant

The Hamilton Restaurant had a great run for sixteen years at 933 Conner Street and closed in 2018, as owners Clyde Worley (the chef) and Vanita Clements (the pastry chef) announced their retirement. The Hamilton was known for its classic approach to dining—escargot, beef stroganoff, baked brie and lamb chops. Their desserts were extraordinary; folks came from miles around for the freshly baked red velvet and hummingbird cakes.

Wimpy's Grill

Originally opened in the 1940s with the grand name Wimpy's Palace, this place was also known over the years as simply Wimpy's and, ultimately, Wimpy's Grill. Regardless of the name, it was a popular gathering spot for many years, serving breakfast, lunch and dinner (it was open until the scandalously late hour of midnight). Located at 198 N. Ninth Street, it was conveniently adjacent to the Diana Theater. Wimpy's was originally owned and operated by John Hall, who also owned the 500 Bar and the Hall Music Company (which was responsible for the many coin-operated jukeboxes around the county). Hall sold Wimpy's to Mitch Pass in 1964, who ran it along with his wife, Patty, until 1970, when it was closed and the building was razed to make room for the Noblesville Bus Station.

FISHERS

Because Fishers is the younger sibling to the other communities in Ham[illegible] County, it simply does not have the long history of restaurants fro[illegible] gone by that the others do. In fact, the most common remark o[illegible]

The Fishers Switch stop on the Interurban Railroad, late 1800s. *Courtesy of Hamilton East Public Library, Joe Roberts Collection.*

about any business district in Fishers is, "I remember, not too long ago, when this whole stretch was nothing but cornfields as far as the eye could see."

The good news is that the culinary scene in Fishers has blossomed exponentially in the last several years and continues to evolve at an astonishing rate along with the growth of both the population and the demand for good, local food. Under the guidance of Fishers' first mayor, Scott Fadness, the culinary scene, along with arts and commerce, is exploding, making Fishers a place to watch in the years to come.

Fionn McCool's

Formerly located at 8211 E. 116th Street, Fionn McCool's served some traditional Irish cuisine, such as shepherd's pie and Irish soda bread, but some dishes were completely off the map—for example, bacon-wrapped bananas. The menu was rounded out with sandwiches and pasta dishes, and live Celtic music was featured on Saturday nights.

Persimmons

Rising up from the sea of diners, chicken places and burger joints in Fishers in the late 1990s, Persimmons Restaurant at Conner Prairie, at 13400 Allisonville Road, definitely turned some heads. In an August 1999 article, *Indianapolis Monthly*'s Julia Spalding swooned over chef Jeffrey Jackson's riffs on modernized comfort food. The first real fine-dining restaurant in Fishers, it featured dishes such as fried green tomatoes topped with crawfish remoulade, pork tenderloin medallions with apple cider syrup, dry-rubbed duck on a bed of polenta with a golden raisin puree, wood-fired pizzas and prime rib with sweet corn–studded whipped potatoes (and, of course, persimmon pudding for dessert, topped with Chantilly cream and brown butter caramel sauce). The décor, however, was not as forward-thinking as the menu, with Shaker-style chairs and fieldstone walls. Spalding described it as "a cross between a ski lodge and a Cracker Barrel." The average price of entrées was around twenty-three dollars.

CARMEL

Barbieri Coast

When Barbieri Coast opened on Carmel's Main Street in 1970, it was unlike anything anyone in Carmel had ever seen. Larry Barbieri (pronounced "Barbary,") who was in his twenties at the time, took over the former Whittaker's Steakhouse. In homage to the Barbary Coast, he had a large pirate sign made for the entrance. The space had a very long bar that did not allow for a spacious dining room, so he decided to cut it down in size. When Barbieri Coast first opened, they were serving breakfast, lunch and dinner, and Barbieri was there for nearly twenty hours every day.

"I literally lived there for six months," Barbieri recalled. "I slept in a booth. But after about six months of this, Tony Mosconi came in one night. Tony had been the maître d' at La Tour downtown, which was a pretty big deal. Tony said, 'You're working too hard for not enough profit. Why don't you up the game around here a bit?'"

Mosconi proceeded to teach Barbieri how to make chateaubriand for two (for $14.95), twin lobster tails (for $10.95) and Steak Diane, along with desserts and drinks flambéed tableside. They brought in white linen tablecloths and turned Barbieri Coast into an upscale supper club with live

A HISTORY OF INDIANA LIQUOR LAWS

Proprietors in the hospitality industry in Indiana have long struggled with overreaching, arcane liquor laws, some of which remain on the books today. Here are some highlights of liquor laws that impacted Hoosiers' rights to imbibe and owners' rights to serve alcohol.

1816: Alcohol sales on Sundays are prohibited
1832: A "minor" is defined as eighteen years old or younger
1855: Indiana institutes its own short-lived, statewide Prohibition sixty-five years ahead of the national ban
1859: Alcohol sales are banned on Election Day until after all polls have closed
1875: "Habitual drunkards" are prohibited from purchasing alcohol after written notice proclaiming them as such from a wife, child, parent or sibling
1910: Townships and counties could vote to go dry; seventy of Indiana's ninety-two counties did so
1918: The law requires a street-facing window in all bars
1933: The ban on Sunday sales is lifted
1934: A "minor" is redefined as twenty-one years old or younger
1935: The ban on Sunday sales is reinstated
1941: Female bartenders are prohibited
1967: The ban on female bartenders is revoked
2010: The law requires all purchasers of alcohol to show proof of age
2011: The 2010 law is amended to require anyone who "appears under the age of 40" to show proof of age

music and dancing. The Indianapolis high rollers started coming in, and the tide turned for Barbieri Coast.

Barbieri's most vivid memory of opening the restaurant, though, was dealing with the alcoholic beverage commission and working around Indiana's arcane liquor laws.

"There were three things that just blew my mind," said Barbieri. "One, we had to have a matron on duty to make sure that the dancers weren't dancing too close together. Two, women were not allowed to sit at the bar. And here's the best part, and I swear I'm not making this up: We had to have a thirty-six-by-thirty-six-inch window up front where you could see into the bar from the street. When I asked why, the excise officer said, 'So that women can look in and see if their husbands are sitting at the bar.' There was apparently no way around it, so we put the damn window in."

Brown's Drugstore

Lots of Carmel folks talked about Brown's Drugstore, but little of its history is recorded. It was a gathering place to discuss the events of the day for much of Carmel up until the late 1940s and early '50s. It was located in Carmel's hub at the intersection of Range Line Road and Main Street and would later become Gilbert's Drugstore.

Brown's Drugstore in Carmel, circa 1920. *Courtesy of the Carmel Clay Historical Society.*

Dairy Queen

Cindy Dunkerly Kemna (*left*) and Waneta Randall Dunkerly of the original Dairy Queen in Carmel. *Photo provided.*

The Dairy Queen in Carmel was a pretty big deal when it opened. Don and Waneta Dunkerly opened it in May 1960 along with two other couples, whom they eventually bought out, becoming the sole owners. Waneta remembers lines out the door and busloads of kids clamoring for a large vanilla cone, which sold for a hefty twenty-five cents.

"Back in those days, there weren't many other restaurants in town other than Toot's Drive-In," Waneta recalled. "So, we were pretty much the only game in town when we opened. We stayed busy seven days a week. All the baseball teams came in after their games, and the high school kids hung out there all the time. They didn't cause any trouble, though, and for a lot of them, we were their first job. I still keep in touch with plenty of them. Eventually, Don even built a miniature golf course there, too. We made a lot of memories there for many Carmel families, including our own."

Waneta recalled that banana splits were their best seller, at forty-five cents each, and kiddie cones (also very popular with their canine customers) were a nickel. If you were looking for something with a bit more sustenance, a hot dog was twenty cents, and it could be upgraded to a chili dog for five more cents. The joint was so jumpin' on the weekends that the Dunkerlys decided to start having live music. They brought an organ from home and hired local keyboardist Carolyn Pfotenhauer to play. After a grand sixteen-year run, the Dunkerlys sold the Dairy Queen to new owners and retired from the business.

Don's Place

There's not a lot of information available on Don's Place, but several Carmel residents remember their grandfathers having lunch there almost every day.

Don's Place in Carmel, circa 1950. *Courtesy of the Carmel Clay Historical Society.*

Illusions Restaurant Magical

Illusions Restaurant Magical was located at 969 Keystone Way North and owned by Pat Baker. The magic began as you entered—you had to pull a sword out of a stone to open the front door. Tableside magic accompanied your dinner. The food was widely reported to be secondary to the name, and the restaurant struggled due to its tucked-away location as well as the departure, in 1999, of then–general manager Jim Tucker and head magician Dan Dygert as they left to open their own magical destination in downtown Indianapolis called Magic Moments. Illusions ultimately closed its doors in 2003 after a fifteen-year run.

MCL Cafeteria

This company was founded in Indianapolis in 1950 by Charles McGaughney and George Laughner. It was originally called McLaugner's Cafeteria but was later shortened to simply MCL Cafeteria. Today, the chain has grown to twenty locations in Indiana, Illinois and Ohio. The Carmel location remains in Merchant's Square, which was built in 1970 and remodeled in the mid-1990s.

Steckley's Olde House

Owned and operated by Jim and Virginia Steckley in the 1970s, Steckley's Olde House was a great spot on Range Line Road for melt-in-your-mouth ribs as well as chicken and steak. The building still stands today and is now home to a thrift shop.

Steckley's Olde House in Carmel, late 1970s. *Courtesy of the Carmel Clay Historical Society.*

The Glass Chimney

In 1976, the culinary landscape in Carmel was dramatically altered when chef Dieter Puska came on the scene and opened the Glass Chimney. Now, instead of choosing between beef tips, Salisbury steak and fried chicken, Carmel diners found themselves torn between escargot "bourguinonne," steak tartare, Dover sole and roast duckling. Fresher fish could not be found in Carmel, as Puska installed a fish tank expressly to serve a French dish called "trout au bleu," in which very fresh trout is quickly poached in court bouillon and turns a dramatic bright blue. It was spectacularly presented and served with a cheesecloth-wrapped lemon half.

A paradigm shift occurred as patrons who had been accustomed to steakhouses passing for fine dining entered the hushed environs on Old Meridian Street, and maître d' Gabriel Piron guided them to their tables and gently placed their napkins on their laps. The prices were on a new level, too, with appetizers ranging anywhere from nine to thirteen dollars

HAMILTON COUNTY FOOD PIONEER CHEF DIETER PUSKA

Dieter Puska came to the United States from Austria in 1967. He had been hired by the Comisar family to work in their Cincinnati restaurant, Maisonette. But when he arrived, Maisonette was closed for remodeling, so he was sent to work at the King Cole restaurant in Indianapolis instead. In his early travels in the United States, he befriended another promising, young Austrian chef by the name of Wolfgang Puck, who, at the time, was working at La Tour in downtown Indianapolis.

"I arrived in the United States with a wife, a child and a couple of suitcases," Puska said. "I worked my way up in the kitchens and eventually became the executive chef at Chanteclair. They left me alone, and I could do what I wanted, but it was always my dream to have my own place."

In 1975, he took over the lease of a ladies' tearoom, located in a strip mall, called the Glass Chimney. He wanted to change the name but couldn't afford a new sign. Loyal patrons followed him from Chanteclair, and he soon outgrew the tearoom space. Around the corner, a restaurant had just gone bankrupt—a place called Mike Tamer's Old World Restaurant. Puska snapped up the equipment, took over the lease and moved into the space at 12901 Old Meridian Street.

Puska was a relentless perfectionist who insisted that both service and food preparation be done in the classic European style. Local cooks clamored for the opportunity to work under the tutelage of the demanding chef, and Puska's kitchen became the gold standard for how a kitchen and dining room should be run.

Dieter Puska, chef/owner of the Glass Chimney in Carmel. *Courtesy of the* Current.

"I was known to be pretty tough," Puska said, with a twinkle in his eye. "But I was fair. I just couldn't tolerate people not trying their best or making excuses or being late. But I never asked anyone to do something I wouldn't do myself."

There were no written recipes in the kitchen of the Glass Chimney. Puska himself taught every dish to every cook who was responsible for making it, while maître d' Gabriel Piron taught the dining room team of captains, front waiters, back waiters and bussers how to properly take care of guests.

When Puska untied his apron strings for the last time in 2008, it was the end of an era. His legacy lives on as his protégés moved on to open their own restaurants. Puska still lives in Carmel. As he reflects on the culinary scene today, he draws a musical analogy: "Some of the chefs today are doing rap. They put stuff together to try and be outrageous, but eventually it has nothing to do with music anymore. Some of them, though, I look at their menus and think, 'I wish I'd thought of that.' But I did the best I could."

and entrées tipping the scales near forty dollars. The dining public was not deterred; the Glass Chimney was wildly successful.

Despite the loyal following the Glass Chimney developed, customers also longed for the same delicious food in a more casual setting. In response to this, Puska opened Deeter's Nip and Nasch, a more pub-like place next door. (He chose to spell his name differently on the new place, as he was afraid folks would think that it was intended for diners who happened to be on a diet).

With Piron, Puska also opened Deeter and Gabe's restaurant in a strip mall on the northwest side of Indianapolis. That space is now occupied by the esteemed Oakley's Bistro.

In 2008, Puska decided it was time to hang up his chef's coat and retire. His then–chef de cuisine, Adam Waldrip, took over for him. But, the Glass Chimney was not the same without Puska, and it finally closed its doors in 2010. The space languished for many years but was given a new life when Cunningham Restaurant Group opened Bru Burger there in 2016.

Tin Star Jail

If you really wanted to be alone with a date or simply liked feeling wanted and dangerous, you would have enjoyed an intimate meal in a jail cell in this themed restaurant on Range Line Road just north of 116th Street. Jail-themed restaurants like Tin Star Jail were popular across the country in the late 1990s and early 2000s.

Toot's Drive-In

This popular hangout on the east side of Range Line Road south of Main Street thrived in the late 1950s and early '60s. When Toot's Drive-In closed, the space would later become home to another popular Carmel eatery called Thornberry's. Today, it's a Mexican restaurant called Cancun.

Whittaker's Steakhouse

Longtime Carmel residents remember Whittaker's Steakhouse on Main Street, which was owned by Emor and Betty Whittaker. The bar was a social center of town, and it was a popular hangout in the 1960s. After Larry Barbieri bought it in the late 1960s, it became Barbieri Coast.

WESTFIELD

Pickett's Cafeteria

Housed in a building that was once Funderburgh's Grocery Store, Pickett's Cafeteria was owned and operated by Bernie and Mary Gibbs Pickett and flourished on the downtown square in Westfield for many years. The space is currently home to Erika's Place and Jan's Village Pizza. Mary Gibbs Pickett died in 1999 at the age of ninety-five after having retired to Naples, Florida.

Lifelong Westfield resident Rachel Merrill remembers dining at Pickett's with her family every Sunday. "Oh, there was everything there you'd ever

Pickett's Cafeteria in Westfield, circa 1960. *Courtesy of the Westfield Washington Historical Society and Museum.*

want to eat. Salisbury steak, chicken and noodles, Jell-O® salad. All of the food was delicious and made from scratch. I remember, in particular, the blackberry pie. Actually, what I remember most about it was dropping a piece as I was putting it on my tray, and what a mess it made! But Pickett's was the place to go, and it was always packed."

OTHER HAMILTON COUNTY COMMUNITIES

Fletchers of Atlanta

Fletchers of Atlanta was an upscale restaurant that was open from the late 1990s to the early 2000s. It was owned by Fletcher Boyd, who had originally opened a restaurant in downtown Indianapolis but relocated farther north to avoid the big-city rent. One of the coolest things about Fletchers was that it was accessible from the Fishers Dinner Train, which transported patrons from Fishers to Atlanta with appetizers included in the ticket price and a cash bar. The menu was limited but included entrée choices such as chicken saltimbocca and halibut with a tropical citrus salsa as well as a special dessert called Russian cream, which was served in a champagne flute.

The extremely eclectic atmosphere included a large wall painting that, when studied closely, revealed itself as consisting of various nude body parts, and the menu descriptions included the words "phallic" and "road kill."

Bub's Big Ugly Burger—to date, only four people have finished it. *Photo provided.*

The hot air balloon at Conner Prairie soars over the historic Conner House. *Courtesy of Connor Prairie.*

Above: Italian sausage–stuffed dates with bacon and romesco sauce at J. Razzo's 2 in Westfield. *Photo provided.*

Left: Fresh pasta is made in-house at Convivio in Carmel. *Photo by author.*

Left: Old-school swank at Matteo's Ristorante Italiano on the square in Noblesville. *Photo by author.*

Below: Downtown Fishers in 2018. *Courtesy of the City of Fishers.*

Above: A welcoming sign in the parking lot of Bonge's Tavern in Perkinsville. *Photo by author.*

Left: House-smoked salmon with traditional accompaniment at Bonge's Tavern in Perkinsville. *Photo by author.*

Grilled Fischer Farms pork chop with grilled polenta, roasted Brussels sprouts and raspberry coulis from Upland Brewing Company's Carmel Tap House. *Photo provided.*

Broccoli Bill's Gray Road Market in Noblesville. *Photo by author.*

The classic burger from Bru Burger in Carmel. *Photo provided.*

Breaded tenderloin sandwich, smoked wings, tacos and the manly wedge salad from Four Day Ray in Fishers. *Photo provided.*

Above: An amazing assortment of sushi from Wild Ginger in Fishers. *Photo by author.*

Right: The shakshuka at Carmel's Eggshell Bistro—a Moroccan dish of tomato, onion, garlic, kale and blistered cherry tomatoes topped with a baked hen's egg and chèvre and accompanied by a grilled baguette. *Courtesy of Larry Hanes.*

Above: The funky and fun atmosphere at Big Dog's Smokehouse in Cicero. *Photo provided.*

Left: The Mediterranean grain bowl at MashCraft Brewery in Fishers. *Photo by author.*

Right: The pastry case at the fun and funky Soho Café in Carmel. *Photo by author.*

Below: Locally brewed Big Lug beer is featured at Sahm's Ale House in Carmel. *Photo provided.*

Left: Avocado toast from Café Patachou in Carmel. *Photo provided.*

Below: Fresh spring rolls at the Asian Grill on the square in Noblesville. *Photo provided.*

Above: The bison meatloaf with honey-chipotle barbeque sauce at Woody's Library in Carmel. *Photo provided.*

Left: The dolsot bibim bop at Café Korea in Fishers. *Photo by Abby David.*

Plenty of books are available to help while away the hours while sipping craft beer at the Books & Brews in Carmel. *Photo by author.*

Fresh peaches in season at Stuckey Farm Market in Sheridan. *Photo provided.*

The world-famous St. Elmo's shrimp cocktail, which will hopefully be found at The Yard Culinary District in Fishers. *Photo provided.*

Flatbread pizza at Michaelangelo's Italian Bistro in Noblesville. *Photo provided.*

Above: The bakery counter at Tina's Tea Room in Carmel. *Photo provided.*

Left: The side of Bonge's Tavern in Perkinsville pays homage to Red Gold tomatoes, which are packaged in Indiana. *Photo by author.*

Homemade peach jam made from the bounty of Indiana's farmers' markets. *Photo by author.*

Ginger chicken and tofu with basil sauce enjoyed al fresco at Thai Kitchen in Fishers. *Photo by author.*

A gorgeous sushi platter garnished with a delicate orchid blossom from Wild Ginger on 116th Street in Fishers. *Photo by author.*

A flight of craft beers from Taxman in Fortville. *Photo by author.*

GASTRONOMICAL GHOSTS

While many eateries housed in historic buildings in Hamilton County are believed to be haunted, Jan's Village Pizza is one of the most widely acknowledged by patrons and staff alike. Bernie Pickett, the owner of Pickett's Cafeteria, is believed to be the culprit.

According to local ghost hunters Michael and Nicole Kobrowski, founders of Historic Indiana Ghost Walks and Tours, unexplained disturbances abound at the building at 108 S. Union Street in Westfield. A television photographer who was there filming a segment in the upstairs space claimed to have become inexplicably immobilized and then pressed against a wall near the stairway as though she were being pushed down the stairs and out of the space. She fled down the steps and refused to return. Cooks regularly report hearing voices in the kitchen, and one employee reported that a pitcher flew off a shelf and nearly hit her in the head when she dared to state that she didn't believe in the ghost. Female waitstaff report ghostly whispers in their ears and the sensation of breathing on the backs of their necks or whispers in their ears. The owners have periodically seen a man standing at the corner of the building who disappears when approached, and muddy prints of both a man's shoes and a dog's paws sometimes appear in the kitchen. The basement features a tunnel that connects with another basement doorway across the street, and it's speculated that it was probably a part of the Underground Railroad.

In Carmel, if you happen to be lingering over after-dinner coffee late at night at Woody's Library, keep one eye open for the ghost of Isaac Bales, the former janitor of the Carnegie Library. He's been spotted amongst the shelves many times over the years. Many of the employees there refuse to go upstairs alone toward the end of the night.

The Anvil Inn: Cicero

The Anvil Inn was a legendary steakhouse that operated for nearly twenty-five years in the sleepy burg of downtown Cicero. It drew steak aficionados from all over the greater Indianapolis area and beyond. The building dates to 1865 and had housed a horse livery, a gas station and a tool implement shop before becoming a restaurant. The original owners were Bob and

Cathy Durst. When the Dursts decided to retire, they were approached by a developer who wanted to tear the building down to erect a Walgreens. The historic building was saved in the nick of time by another husband-and-wife team, James Dupont and Kimberli Baker, who bought the business and continued the restaurant's grand tradition for a few more years. Ultimately, they closed the restaurant, and it briefly housed a motorcycle shop until yet another husband-and-wife team brought a restaurant back into the space. Cicero natives Chris and Cheryl Faulkner bought it in 2011, and it has housed Big Dog's Smokehouse (named for the Hamilton Heights High School football team) ever since.

4

NOBLESVILLE

Can't-Miss Destinations and Culinary Superstars

Because Noblesville has the longest history of all the cities and towns in Hamilton County, it has easy-to-find destinations that appeal to foodies and historians alike. The picturesque courthouse square is framed with charming, delectable and diverse culinary establishments that are housed in ornate historic buildings. The eateries of today certainly have more sophisticated offerings than the taverns and coffee shops that came before them, but Noblesville has done a marvelous job of preserving the history of its city. The buildings have been lovingly maintained and restored. Walking into many of the storefronts on the square feels like walking back into the 1800s, when these buildings housed the young county's first banks, theaters and sundry stores.

ON THE COURTHOUSE SQUARE

One of the most iconic restaurants on the courthouse square is **Rosie's Place**, located at 68 N. Ninth Street. In the 1960s, the building housed Elliott's Drug Store. In 2010, husband-and-wife team Debbi and Michael Bourgerie worked with Charlie Elliott, the former pharmacist there, to restore the building to its original glory, and Rosie's Place opened its doors.

Because Debbi is a constant presence in both the kitchen and the dining room, she's often called "Rosie," and she typically doesn't correct folks. But Rosie is actually Debbi's grandmother, and Debbi uses Rosie's recipes to make nearly everything on the menu from scratch, with love, every day.

Rosie's Place is pretty much packed daily from the time they open to the time they close. The creative breakfast and lunch menus change with the seasons, and they utilize locally grown ingredients whenever possible. At breakfast, they offer interesting options such as a veggie hash—an amazing compilation of quinoa, sweet potatoes, onions, Brussels sprouts, mushrooms, spinach and sage topped with poached eggs, hollandaise and reduced balsamic vinegar. The lunch menu has several great vegetarian options, including a portobello mushroom burger. They also offer gluten-free toast and pancakes. But lest it sound too healthy, their baked goods are insanely good and worth every calorie. Their "ooey gooey butter cookie" will rock your world. They've recently opened Rosie's Place locations in Zionsville and Carmel as well.

You'll feel as though you've stepped back in time to the grand days of supper clubs and jazz when you enter the swanky confines of **Matteo's Ristorante Italiano**, located just a few doors down from Rosie's Place. Matteo's has been a mainstay on the Noblesville square since 2003, when it was opened by Salerno, Italy native Matteo di Rosa. Matteo doesn't own it anymore—in 2016, he sold it to Joelcir Antunes and Adson Franco—but the name lives on.

The glorious building was constructed in the 1880s and has been home to a cigar store, a billiards hall, a confectionery and a J.C. Penney store from 1948 through the late 1980s. The décor pays homage to the room's noble history with crystal chandeliers, curving booths and a magnificent staircase that leads up to a second-floor private dining room.

The food is old-school, classic Italian. One of their signature dishes, the penne norcia—with house-made Italian sausage, mushrooms, garlic, Parmesan cheese and a tomato cream sauce—is a must-try. For dessert, the delizia limone—a delightful, citrusy version of tiramisu with limoncello-soaked ladyfingers layered with lemon pastry cream—is divine.

Helen Worley Cromell (a.k.a. Dirty Helen) was one of Hamilton County's most notorious women. Originally from Cicero, she allegedly had connections to Al Capone and was a madam and tavern owner (and, according to some accounts, also a bank robber). **Barley Island Brewery**, located along the southern end of the square at 639 Conner Street, pays homage to Cromell with their Dirty Helen Brown Ale—a top-notch, smooth and nutty ale with a fabulous label depicting Helen in a jaunty bowler hat.

Barley Island owners Jeff and Linda Eaton opened the doors in 1999 and expanded into bottling their beer in 2003. The menu is straightforward bar fare, but many items have an Irish tilt. You'll find bangers and mash,

The entryway at Barley Island Brewery in downtown Noblesville. *Photo by Abby David.*

a hearty Irish stew called Dublin coddle, fish and chips and, of course, a breaded pork tenderloin sandwich. The historic building is worth a visit, as it sits in the Noblesville Commercial Historic District. Known for decades as the Livery Building, it once stabled horses and served for years as a beer distribution warehouse.

If you happen to be in the mood for Asian food, there's one option on the square for you, and it's a great one. **Asian Grill**, at 74 N. Ninth Street, lines right up in a row with Rosie's Place and Matteo's. The Asian Grill offers pan-Asian cuisine in a cozy setting. A far cry from a typical Chinese restaurant or

Courtney's Kitchen in Noblesville. *Photo provided.*

sushi bar, it's a completely unique concept in Hamilton County. It's a casual Asian bistro that offers a wide array of freshly made Asian dishes influenced by Japanese, Chinese, Korean, Thai and Indian cooking methods. The vegetable samosas with cilantro chutney are amazing.

Courtney's Kitchen, at 654 Logan Street, is family-owned by brother-and-sister duo Cass and Carrie Courtney. Just off the northwest corner of the square, Courtney's Kitchen offers breakfast on the weekends, with biscuits and gravy and novel offerings, such as all-you-can-eat pancakes, complemented by Bloody Marys and mimosas. The lunch and dinner menus offer stick-to-your-ribs, home-cooked cuisine such as beef Manhattans and barbecue chicken.

The iconic sign hanging on the corner at the intersection of Eighth and Conner Streets shows wear and tear but still shines bright. The stately building at 809 Conner Street was constructed in 1883 by the Lowther family and originally opened as Lowther's Shoe Store. The spot has been home to a café with various owners since 1932 and is currently home to the **Sunrise Café at Uptown**. A spartan diner décor jazzed up by jukeboxes has set the stage over the years for predictable comfort food, bottomless cups of coffee and freshly baked cinnamon rolls and muffins. A spoonful of their house-made strawberry jam can brighten even the darkest of days.

Left: The original Uptown Café sign still hangs over the Sunrise Café at Uptown. *Photo by author.*

Right: Syd's Bar, with the coolest neon sign in Hamilton County. *Photo by author.*

If you love classic neon signs and dive bars, a stop into Syd's is essential. While it's recently been renamed **Syd's Fine Food and Spirits**, the original name of **Syd's Bar** is much more apropos. The kitsch factor in here is off the charts. If you're looking for an upscale dinner, this isn't the place for you, but if dive bars are your thing, you'll be sad if you miss it. You'll feel like you've stepped back in time when you walk in the door—because you have. The building at 808 Logan Street was opened as a tavern in the historic J.L. Evans building by Walter Carey and Sid Gill in 1945 and originally offered lodging on its upper floors. Syd's offers burgers, salads and sandwiches, and locals swear by the fried catfish sandwich and Philly steak.

There's nothing like a funky, locally owned coffee shop to round out a cool dining district, and **Noble Coffee and Tea Company** at 933 Logan Street fits that bill. It's a big space with a cool urban vibe and is a great spot for a time-out during an adventure around the Noblesville square. They roast their own beans and offer a nice selection of pastries. There's a nice little outdoor seating area, as well, which is perfect for admiring the view of the gorgeous courthouse square and soaking up the local culture.

OFF THE SQUARE

The Wolf family pretty much has Hamilton County covered, with restaurants in Carmel, Fishers, Westfield and Noblesville. Wolfie's restaurants, as well as their latest concept, the Italian House on Park, are a family affair—they have been owned and operated by husband and wife Scott and Nyla Wolf, along with their children Alec and Ansley, since they opened the first location in 2004. This particular location, **Wolfie's Northern Woods Grill**, is located at 20999 Hague Road on the lovely Morse Reservoir and features stunning waterfront views from the huge back deck. While it's nearly impossible for the food to be as spectacular as the scenery, the fish and chips are killer, and the mountain ridge ribs are heaven.

The Caplinger family opened their first combination fish market, butcher shop and restaurant years ago in Indianapolis. They've since expanded to Noblesville and Whitestown, near Zionsville. Andrew Caplinger comes by his title of fishmonger honestly—his family has been in the fish business for a combined 125 years. He and his dad, Nick, oversee the operations at **Caplinger's Fresh Catch and Cuts** at 15009 Gray Road. The atmosphere is casual, and the portions are bountiful. If you're looking for

The cozy private dining room at Wolfie's Grill in Carmel. *Photo provided.*

Michaelangelo's Italian Bistro, previously the home of Clancy's in Noblesville. *Photo by author.*

some fresh fish to take home and prepare, there's virtually nothing you can't find here, and if they don't have it, they'll get it for you. While you might be delighted with their selection of fresh salmon, tuna, swordfish and king crab legs, you'll be amazed to also find escargot, frog legs, octopus and alligator tail. (Author's note: Since the writing of this book, Caplinger's has closed their Noblesville location. However, plentiful fresh catch still abounds at their Indianapolis, Zionsville and Lawrence locations.)

If you look closely, you can still see the vestiges of the Clancy's drive-thru when you look at the facade of **Michaelangelo's Italian Bistro** at 550 Westfield Road. Clancy's reigned supreme in this location in the 1960s and '70s. Although it's still in the Clancy's family, this hip, newly redesigned spot is a far cry from the fifteen-cent burger joint that once served patrons clamoring for quick and inexpensive burgers and fries. Today, executive chef and partner Alex Cunion presents authentic Italian flavors that pair marvelously with a thoughtful and reasonably priced wine list, craft cocktails and long list of local beers. They also prominently feature local produce and artisan foods, including Smoking Goose capocollo.

Jeff Eaton, the owner of Barley Island on the square, expanded his beer empire with **Deer Creek Brewery** at 17661 Cumberland Road. Eaton partnered with Eric Smith to open this massive production facility. Both have long histories in the business world but are passionate brewers who wanted

Deer Creek Brewery in Noblesville. *Photo by Betsy Wood.*

to collaborate. Deer Creek Brewery is housed in a thirteen-thousand-square-foot building that was previously home to a meatpacking facility that once processed one hundred thousand pounds of bacon a week. It's now equipped to brew four thousand barrels of beer a year and growing fast. There's no food offered in the tasting room, but you're welcome to bring in food or order carry-out from any nearby restaurant.

Bill Weghurst opened **Broccoli Bill's Fresh Produce and Specialty Grocery** at 15009 Gray Road in 1994; it started out as a simple farm market and has grown significantly since then. It features many locally sourced fruits and vegetables, including tomatoes from Diener Farms in Whitestown and sweet corn from Watermans Farm Market and Lightfoot Farms in Tipton. They also sell Gonella Bread and Boar's Head lunchmeat and offer a nice selection of prepared salads and meals that include lasagna, pulled pork and meatloaf. It's a great spot to sit and have lunch, and there's a lovely screened-in patio for al fresco dining in the warmer months. Their signature broccoli salad is legendary around these parts. It's mayonnaise-based, but the addition of both balsamic and apple cider vinegar gives it a lovely zing.

The Russell family has owned the farmland that is home to **Russell Farms Pumpkin Patch**, at 12290 E. 191st Street, for over fifty years. They started the pumpkin patch in 2002. This is a great place to visit year-round, with farm exhibits and a petting zoo featuring miniature Jersey cows, sheep, pygmy goats, turkeys, peacocks, ducks, chickens and more. There are two country stores offering fudge, apple butter, candy and apple cider. Visitors can wander through either a five- or ten-acre corn maze or take a ride on a hay wagon. And, if all this adventure builds up an appetite, there's a snack shack on-site as well.

5

FISHERS

Can't-Miss Destinations and Culinary Superstars

Did you ever have a cousin who was unbearably awkward and shy when you were growing up but turned out to be a smart and sophisticated grown-up when you saw them at the family reunion? That's Fishers. Most of the credit for that transition from gawky teenager to worldly adult is due to some visionary leadership by Scott Fadness, the first mayor of Fishers, along with other civic and business leaders.

Unlike Noblesville, Fishers does not have a historic town square. In fact, it boasts only a handful of buildings that have any history at all. However, the development that has occurred in the last few years is historic in and of itself. Fishers has become a hotbed for technology businesses. The once-tiny private airport is expanding to accommodate larger multinational organizations that are relocating their headquarters to Fishers. Housing is booming, and in 2017, Fishers was named *Money Magazine*'s "No. 1 Best Place to Live." Although Fishers is much more spread out than the other cities in Hamilton County, a town center has emerged with the new municipal complex on 116th Street that is home to the library, city services, the Saturday farmer's market and a marvelous outdoor music venue called the Nickel Plate Amphitheater.

Fishers was once a bit of a culinary desert. Independent restaurant owners struggled to establish themselves in strip malls, and chains were just not interested because of the lack of population density. How times have changed; Fishers is now home to a thriving culinary scene that features a diverse selection of ethnic restaurants, casual mom-and-pop cafés, a little bit of fine dining and a whole lot of beer! The microbrewery trend is booming in Fishers, so if you're in the mood for a locally brewed malted beverage, Fishers is a great place to start.

MICROBREWERIES AND WINE

The trailblazer in the Fishers microbrew scene was **Books & Brews**. It started out as a dream of owner Jason Wuerfel, who wanted to marry his love for books with his love of beer. Lacking funding to bring his dream to reality, he ran an outrageously successful crowdfunding campaign and parlayed those funds into opening capital. He built all the barstools and tables himself and opened the doors of the first Books & Brews in 2013. The success of this place is a ringing tribute to the power of social media—Wuerfel didn't have an advertising budget, and the storefront has zero visibility, as it's tucked into a strip mall that doesn't face the road just off of Ninety-Sixth Street at 9402 Uptown Drive. Beer lovers found it anyway. Since opening Books & Brews, Wuerfel has doubled the size of the original space and now has a private party room as well a space for live music.

Kids are welcome in the front room, which is an awesome used-book store, where they can sit and read books or play games. Mom and dad can check out literary titles of a different ilk in the back bar, where all the beers feature clever riffs on book names. For example, their signature cream ale is called Cream and Punishment, their chocolate stout is Charlie and the Chocolate Stout and their ale is Clifford, the Big Red Ale.

The menu is mostly just appetizers and sandwiches, but they're really good. They're made with local Smoking Goose meats and served with to-die-for chips from the local Broad Ripple Chip Company. The food items also have fabulous names—sandwiches served on grilled naan are listed in a section entitled "Naan Fiction," their spicy grilled cheese is "Dante's Inferno" and (this one's a little sad) their pulled pork sandwich is named "Babe."

Wuerfel has franchised his concept, and the Books & Brews empire now includes locations in Carmel, Zionsville, Brownsburg, Speedway, Muncie and several Indianapolis locations.

Four Day Ray (FDR) is located in the new municipal complex at 11671 Lantern Road. You really can't miss it, as the adjacent water tower emblazoned with the letters "FDR" is visible from quite far away. The name playfully pays homage to the railroad history of the Nickel Plate District. "Four Day Ray" was the name given to an employee who called off sick one day per week, usually guaranteeing a three-day weekend.

Redemption Alewerks in Fishers.
Photo by author.

This massive, two-level brewery and restaurant was opened in 2016 by Brian Graham, who has a decade of restaurant experience behind him and a long history of brewing beer. It now also features a spacious and cozy beer garden and an upstairs mezzanine that's available for private dining. The menu focuses heavily on smoked food. There are lots of sandwiches and just a few entrées featuring chicken, beef and fish. The spicy pork belly taco is fantastic.

And, of course, there is beer. The Laplander Blonde ale (a "laplander" is a passenger who falls and lands on someone's lap on a crowded train) is citrusy, sweet and slightly acidic—a perfect complement to your meal.

Also in a strip mall—but much more visible than Books & Brews—is **Redemption Alewerks**, located at 7035 E. Ninety-Sixth Street. This is a wonderful, industrial, cheerfully funky space to have lunch or dinner along with a cocktail or beer. It features one of the best brunch menus in Hamilton County. Redemption is a family affair owned by brothers Brandon and Ben Smith along with their cousin Josh. The brewmaster is Cameron Fila. The bookshelves are fully stocked with board games, and there's outdoor seating, so it's a great spot to while away an afternoon.

All the way on the east side of Fishers, you'll find **Wooden Bear Brewing at Geist** at 10150 Brooks School Road. The original Wooden Bear Brewery opened in 2014 in Greenfield in the lovingly restored Gant Opera House building, which was constructed in the late 1800s. The Geist location opened in 2017. Wooden Bear is owned by four partners: Kurt Sundling, Jason Swift, Dan Noah and Brent Sandquist, all IT guys by day. The menu consists of just a few starters, some nice salads and mighty fine pizza. The buffalo chicken pizza, with banana peppers and onions, is fantastic and pairs well with their slightly sweet and citrusy Growl at the Moon Witbier.

Along the well-traveled path of Allisonville Road sits **MashCraft Brewery** (11069 Allisonville Road). MashCraft opened its first location in Greenwood on the south side of Indianapolis. In 2018, it took over the space of the short-lived Heady Hollow Brewery. The owners describe their menu as "elevated pub food," but that's really short-changing it. The menu, by chef Joe Hsu of 5280 Bistro, is interesting and innovative, stretching beyond the usual suspects of burgers and tacos into grain bowls, pastas, house-made soup and charcuterie made with locally produced cheeses and smoked meats. The PB&J sandwich is amazing—it's thinly sliced roasted pork loin with peppered bacon topped with fig and plum jam, all served on a pretzel bun.

If beer isn't your thing, you can find a glass of wine just a few doors down from MashCraft at **Harmony Winery**. It's also along Allisonville Road, but it's tucked back at 7350 Village Square Lane in Suite 200. Owners Kevin and Tatyana Croak have been making wine here in Fishers since 2001. Wine production happens in the back, but there's a cute tasting room up front with a bar, fireplace and comfy seating areas. The Croaks often partner with local caterers and chefs for wine-tasting dinners. Their wines have won numerous awards, and they're generous with their wine knowledge (and their tasting pours). They've recently begun producing port, and their Encore Ruby is lovely.

FINE DINING

Beer and casual dining is certainly abundant in Fishers, but there's one special place that stands alone in the otherwise laid-back scene. In a world of steakhouse chains, **Peterson's**, located at 7690 E. Ninety-Sixth Street, seems to be one of the last independently owned steakhouse concepts that still stands. Owner Joe Peterson opened the doors in 1999 on this clubby, intimate space complete with cozy booths and a lovely private dining room that he's recently remodeled. Peterson's has been listed in the *Indianapolis Monthly*'s "Best Restaurant" issue every year since they've opened and has garnered several *Wine Spectator* awards for their wine list that features more

Peterson's, one of the few locally owned steakhouses in Hamilton County. *Photo by author.*

than four hundred bottles. Peterson's also spotlights local producers through offerings such as Indiana Gunthorp Farms pork loin, which is finished with a marvelous maple-cider glaze. The sweet and salty blue crab–stuffed bacon-wrapped shrimp is also a must-try.

CASUAL EATS

Nestled along the original Nickel Plate Railroad tracks is the **Nickel Plate Bar and Grill** at 8654 E. 116th Street. It's one of the rare historic buildings in central Fishers. It was constructed in the 1880s and originally housed the Parks Place Saloon. While the building was renovated and expanded in 1991, it still boasts the original architectural features, including hardwood floors and exposed brick walls and archways. A cozy outdoor patio allows diners to soak up the historical feel of Old Town Fishers while the new city center thrives just across the street. While many restaurants in central Indiana claim to have the best breaded pork tenderloin sandwich, this version just might take the cake.

Pure Eatery, located at 8235 E. 116th Street, is locally owned by Dave and Courtney Andrus. This is their second location; the original is in Fountain Square on the south side of Indianapolis, and they have also opened a third location in Lafayette. As its name implies, Pure focuses on tasty, clean eating in this cheerful and art-filled space. It's a great place for vegetarians or those who just like to eat healthy. Everything on the menu, including soups and salad dressings, is made from scratch daily. Locally produced Smoking Goose meats are prevalent on the menu, and the entrée section is loaded with excellent fresh fish choices, including sockeye salmon and tuna.

For something slightly more rustic, there's a sister location of Noblesville's **Wolfie's Northern Woods Grill** at 7695 Crosspoint Commons, and **Wolfie's at Geist**, in the space that formerly housed the Bella Vita restaurant, at 11699 Fall Creek Road.

Since 1986, Sahm's restaurants have been ubiquitous throughout Indianapolis and Hamilton County. **Sahm's Restaurant and Pub**, at

The historic Nickel Plate Bar and Grill in Fishers. *Photo by Abby David.*

The interior of Pure Eatery in Fishers. *Photo by Abby David.*

11505 Allisonville Road, is the mothership of that empire. The flagship location has been newly remodeled and feels almost like a supper club with its cushy booths and dark interior, but the menu is strictly comfort food. In essence, it's an upscale diner with great service and a full bar. You might think you're being virtuous by ordering a salad, but it will come with a slice of their famous sour cream coffee cake, and it's a sure bet that you won't send it back. If you're going to eat fried chicken in Hamilton County, this is the place to do it. And then there's the coffee cake. Did we mention the sour cream coffee cake?

The Roost, located at 371 E. 116th Street, is also owned by Sahm's. Opened in 1996, it's a Fishers institution. It's a straight-up dive offering no-nonsense breakfast and lunch at incredibly cheap prices. The warm apple fritters dusted with powdered sugar and served with apple butter will warm your soul, and the Indiana white corn grits—topped with your choice of cheese, bacon or sausage—will stick to your ribs all day.

HAMILTON COUNTY FOOD SUPERSTAR ED SAHM

Ed Sahm. *Photo provided.*

In 1985, Ed Sahm was passing through Fishers when a run-down building, which had housed both a gas station and a bar called McKori's, at the corner of Allisonville Road and 116th Street caught his eye. "I could do something with that building," he thought. Sahm had recently earned his degree in restaurant and hotel management at Purdue University, and he was ready to put that degree into practice. He had an opportunity to join a couple of other guys who wanted to open a restaurant, so he dove in head first. He hasn't come up for air since.

Sahm opened his namesake restaurant in 1986, much to the dismay of the cows that had, up until that time, been grazing undisturbed in the pasture across the street. The parking lot was gravel, he had fewer than twenty employees and the menu and concept were simple: good, quality ingredients and sauces, soups, salad dressings, meatloaf, mashed potatoes and freshly baked breads and desserts made in-house from scratch. Diners came from miles away.

One successful restaurant is enough for many restaurateurs, but Sahm was just getting started. In Fishers, he went on to open a breakfast and lunch joint called The Roost in 1994 (after a failed attempt at a yogurt shop in the space) and Sahm's Bar and Grill at Ninety-Sixth Street and Highway 69 in 2000. Other Sahm's concepts include Rockstone Pizza, Big Lug Canteen and Sahm's Ale House.

"I feed people. That's what I do," said Sahm. "My restaurants are the kinds of places you could eat three times a week. It's just good, wholesome food."

Sahm believes in seeking out locations in areas that need a neighborhood restaurant and becoming entrenched in the community. Most of his restaurants are in spaces where another restaurant has failed. He moves in and works his magic to turn the location around. Since its humble beginnings by the cow pasture in 1986, his restaurant empire has grown to a total of eight restaurants in Hamilton County with another six in Indianapolis, and he now employs nearly six hundred people.

Although the scope of his operation has changed, his philosophy has not.

"My grandparents were farmers in Montgomery County," he said. "They went to the grocery store twice a year, and everything else they ate came from the farm. My love of cooking and my passion for local, fresh ingredients is deeply rooted. I'll always use local ingredients from local growers and producers every chance I get."

ETHNIC DELIGHTS

There are numerous unique and authentic ethnic restaurants in Fishers, and most of them have been around for quite some time. **Café Korea**, at 11003 Allisonville Road, started out as a tiny, family-owned café tucked into a strip mall off 116th Street. They have since outgrown their original location. They moved into a much larger space in 2018. The new space is short on ambiance but long on authentic Korean cuisine and bright, fresh Asian flavors. In traditional Korean style, every order comes complete with a seemingly endless parade of Korean side dishes, including kimchee, the spicy fermented cabbage salad that accompanies most every Korean meal.

You can't eat at a Korean restaurant without having dolsot bibimbap, and theirs is done right. It arrives in a screaming hot stone bowl filled with sushi rice and topped with bulgolgi (Korean barbecued beef) as well as pickled and fresh vegetables and a sunny-side-up egg. The Chilean sea bass is also not to be missed—it's served on a bed of hot stones, and it's perfectly seared, crunchy and caramelized on the outside and buttery, flaky and rich inside.

Just a few storefronts down is **Thai Kitchen** at 11021 Allisonville Road. This is seriously amazing Thai food. The restaurant is family-owned, with a beautiful and intimate dining area (and a very nice patio in the summertime). It's packed at lunchtime but worth the wait. Start with the Chiang Mai larb salad. It's offered with a choice of ground chicken or tofu; go with the chicken and order it mild. Their medium is not for the faint of heart, and the hot is downright dangerous. For the main course, the pad thai is fantastic—hands down, the best in Hamilton County.

Thai Kitchen in Fishers. *Photo by author.*

If you're hungry for sushi, **Wild Ginger**, located at 8235 E. 116th Street (in the Fishers Town Commons), is the place to go. There just aren't a ton of great sushi places in Fishers that have stood the test of time, so this place is special for that alone. But it's also a beautiful space with genuinely friendly staff and reasonably priced, very fresh sushi. If at all possible, take a group and try one of the sushi combination platters. They're spectacularly presented and a great way to try a variety of Wild Ginger's offerings.

One last Asian restaurant to note is **Main Street Poké** at 8594 E. 116th Street, Suite 30. This restaurant opened in Carmel, and the owners quickly replicated the concept in Fishers due to the huge, loyal following they created. In a world of less-than-healthy fast food, Main Street Poké gives a person hope that food can be fast, fresh, healthy and delicious. If you've never tried poké, you're in for a treat; the traditional Hawaiian dish is offered much like a Chipotle for fresh fish—you pick your toppings and choose your own adventure. You start with a base of white rice, brown rice or lettuce and then add a protein of either raw or cooked fish (or you could choose the caramelized Spam if you really want authentic Hawaiian food). Then, you add in a sweet or spicy sauce and fresh vegetables to your heart's

St. Yared, the only Ethiopian restaurant in Hamilton County. *Photo by author.*

desire. It's absolutely divine and different every time you go. There are a million amazing combinations to try, but here's a great one: a brown rice bowl with marinated tuna topped with spicy aioli, ginger, mango, edamame and fried onion.

One might not expect to find an authentic Ethiopian restaurant in Fishers, but **St. Yared Ethiopian Cuisine and Coffeehaus** at 11210 Fall Creek Road will dissuade any skeptics. In addition to the highly specialized and ritualistic Ethiopian coffee service, St. Yared is a great stop for a hearty, flavorful meal. Husband and wife Haile and Etenesh Abebe opened the restaurant in 2013. Etenesh's hands touch every dish that leaves the kitchen. Her mother and sisters, who still live in Ethiopia, make berbere, the unique and essential spice required for authentic Ethiopian food, each month and ship it to Fishers.

Not sure what to try? If you're a fan of lamb, the Ye-beg Wot is amazing; it's a spicy lamb stew with onion, garlic and ginger. If you don't love lamb, variations on this dish are available with beef or chicken. There's a vegetarian version, as well, made with lentils. And, of course, you must have coffee service.

A LITTLE SOMETHING SWEET

If you see a white delivery van driving around Hamilton County adorned with a giant, winged, pink cupcake on top, follow it to the **Flying Cupcake Bakery** at 13180 Market Square Drive, Suite 101. Flying Cupcake Bakery has been providing mile-high sweet treats in Hamilton County and around the Circle City area since owner Kate Bova Drury opened her first location in 2007. It was the first cupcake shop in the state. Whether you're vegan, gluten-free or gluten-loving, there's a cupcake here for you. The Bee's Knees is a particular favorite. It's a delicate ginger, honey and pear cupcake topped with honey buttercream frosting.

THE FUTURE OF FISHERS DINING

The Yard Culinary District project was launched in 2017 with a mission to foster even more development of independent restaurants in Fishers. The food-centric, open-air mall will ultimately feature around fifteen restaurants on a seventeen-acre campus that is also slated to have a hotel (with more than two hundred rooms), apartments, retail shops and a center green with open space for live music and festivals. Indianapolis-based **St. Elmo Steakhouse** was among the first to sign on and will debut a new concept named **HC Grill**. Hopefully, the "World Famous" St. Elmo shrimp cocktail, with its legendary sinus-clearing cocktail sauce, will still appear on the menu.

6

CARMEL

Can't-Miss Destinations and Culinary Superstars

Fishers has recently made great strides, but Carmel has been in it to win it in the dining game for a while. Mayor Jim Brainard's vision of a picturesque, walkable city with a European flair has always included courting unique, independently owned restaurants as well as some major-player, upscale chains.

Carmel is constantly developing. Eventually, the Arts and Design District that stretches grandly up and down Main Street will join with the stunning City Center about a mile to the south. It will be connected by a city greenway, which will be home to even more restaurants. Carmel has several must-visit walking and dining destinations.

THE ARTS AND DESIGN DISTRICT

If you only have time to visit one area in Carmel, the Arts and Design District should be it. Park your car anywhere you can find a spot along Main or one of the side streets. Start at one end and work your way up one side and down the other.

On the west end of the district, nestled along the Monon Trail at 210 W. Main Street, sits a cheery-looking institution known as **Bub's Burgers and Ice Cream**. (If you can't find it, look for the friendly policeman statue stopping traffic just out front.) This place is legendary. In the summer months, you can find it by looking for a giant crowd of people waiting for a

Carmel's lovely Arts and Design District, bustling with art galleries, boutiques and independently owned restaurants. *Courtesy of the City of Carmel.*

table. While it was obviously founded as a burger place, top sellers include the chili and their all-Angus beef hot dogs. "Big" is the name of the game at Bub's, so go hungry. Bub's is home to the "Big Ugly" Burger, which is a one-pound burger—and one pound is the cooked weight (which means that uncooked, it's twenty-two ounces of meat). It was featured on the Travel Channel show *Man v. Food*, and to date, only four people have finished it. It comes in at just under twenty dollars for the beef version and nearly thirty dollars for elk. Most diners will opt for the half- or quarter-pounder instead. The obvious choice is a burger, but the mahi mahi sandwich, served on garlic herb focaccia with peach-mango salsa, is also yummy. Whatever you do, save room for ice cream.

Just across the street, **Bazbeaux Pizza** at 111 W. Main Street is also an institution in both Carmel and Indianapolis. Named after the clever court jester turned chef in the court of Lorenzo de Medici, Bazbeaux strives to "continue his philosophy of whimsy, originality and excellence." It's not fancy, but it's fun to sit outside along the trail and watch the runners and pups go by. The Mediterranean pizza—with house-made chorizo, pepperoni, feta, spinach and in-house roasted red peppers—is amazing.

If you find yourself standing next to a statue of a woman carrying a bag loaded with groceries, you've found your way to **Joe's Butcher Shop** and

Joe's Butcher Shop in Carmel is graced by a Seward Johnson sculpture. *Photo by author.*

Joe's Next Door Café, which are also in the building at 111 W. Main Street. Joe's is a fixture on Main Street and offers delectable items such as ground lamb and baseball-sized sea scallops. It's a sweet little gourmet market, and you'll find it hard to resist grabbing extra treats for your basket while you wait for your number to be called. Owner Joe Lazzara has also opened a little café next door that specializes in beautifully made sandwiches and salads, quick meals to go and catering. Locally sourced meat is easy to get here—they work with many local farmers, and they're a great source for grass-fed, natural beef and free-range chicken.

The original **Main Street Poké** is right across the street at 110 W. Main Street. (Check out the details about this place in the Fishers section.)

A little farther east, you'll find one of the pioneer restaurants on Main Street—**Mudbugs Cajun Café** at 20 W. Main. This tiny, brightly colored counter-service café tucked between the numerous art galleries on Main Street has been around for over ten years. Born and raised in Abbeville, Louisiana, owner Roy LeBlanc knows a little bit about Cajun cuisine. He serves up delightful Cajun food in a casual setting fully bedecked with Mardi Gras beads and southern paraphernalia. It's a great spot to grab a quick lunch, dinner or snack while gallery-hopping. The shrimp étouffée is outrageous, and the beignets will melt in your mouth.

Inspired by his wife Laura's generous spirit, Scott Burton, together with his family, opened **Peace Water Winery** at 37 W. Main Street in 2015. The tasting room is stunningly beautiful and features a marvelous outdoor patio in the back for warm-weather al fresco sipping. While the stellar wine is made in California with California grapes, the hospitality is purely Hoosier. You can feel good about buying bottles of wine to take home with you, as you'll receive a token for every bottle purchased and can use those tokens to choose which charity will be the beneficiary of the 50 percent of the sale donated for every bottle sold. No food is served, but you can order carry-out from any one of the wonderful restaurants that line Main Street and enjoy it with your wine.

In any season, their Inspire Rosé is lovely. It's a light, crisp, fruit-forward (but dry) blush with notes of sour cherry, berries, citrus and melon. It's insanely food-friendly—as perfect with your summer caprese as it is with your Thanksgiving turkey. You might want to take a case home with you.

On the east end of Main Street is **Woody's Library** (40 E. Main). Housed in the original Carmel Carnegie Public Library, which was built in 1913, Woody's Library is one of Carmel's oldest family dining establishments. The menu is chef-driven pub fare with lots of vegetarian and gluten-free choices. Eating in the lovingly restored upstairs dining room amongst the book-laden, original library shelves will make you feel as though you've stepped back into the early 1900s.

"Family dining" might imply that the menu is simple. It's not. The sweet and spicy bison meatballs with a honey-chipotle glaze are delicious, and you won't find a more luscious and creamy chicken pot pie; it's studded with peas, green beans, onions, carrots and potatoes and topped with a delicate puff pastry. Vegetarians will love the Tex Mex quinoa tacos with black beans, onions, cilantro, lettuce, tomatoes, jalapeños and sour cream.

Woody's Library in Carmel still has the original bookcases from the Carnegie library. *Photo by author.*

Before you leave Main Street, there's one more place you absolutely must experience. **Tina's Traditional English Tea Room**, at the corner of Main and Rangeline, is an absolutely delightful and authentic English tearoom. It's owned by British expat Tina Jesson, who moved to America from England in 2008. She began by baking scones and selling them at local farmer's markets, but her business has now expanded to two tearooms, with a second location in Columbus. They feature a wide range of loose leaf teas, pastries and a simple but elegant lunch menu. They also offer etiquette classes and themed parties for showers, birthdays and other celebrations. If you want to feel royal, make a reservation for their high tea service. Finger sandwiches and pastries are served on a towering, three-tiered cake stand along with Devonshire clotted cream and, of course, a pot of tea.

Just around the corner is **Blu Moon Café** at 200 S. Rangeline Road. This is Carmel's go-to spot for a quick breakfast or lunch, but it's far from fast food. Located in the Indiana Design Center building, Blu Moon has an artsy, hip and urban feel. The large refrigerated display cases are always packed to the gills, featuring a bounty of imaginative, fresh and delicious house-made salad choices as well as sweets and breakfast items. For breakfast, go with the warm granola with fresh berries and steamed milk. For lunch, the brie and pancetta panini with roasted pears and fresh spinach is divine.

Bub's Café, at 220 Second Street SW, is the sassy younger sister of Bub's Burgers and Ice Cream and is a short walk down the Monon Trail. The décor is warm and cheerful and features a large, sunny deck for al fresco dining and people-watching. Not surprisingly, the "big" theme continues here, so if you happen to wake up starving, head over to Bub's for the "Big Stack"—a mountain of twelve fluffy buttermilk pancakes. If that feels like a bit of a carb overload in the morning (or if you can't find six friends to share it with you), opt for a walking omelet in a warm spinach or tomato tortilla or the quiche of the day. Don't leave without trying the Bub's holes—house-made doughnut holes finished with your choice of cinnamon sugar, powdered sugar, glaze or chocolate.

If you continue south on Rangeline Road, you'll come to a large, older strip mall on the west side of the street. With the glamour of the City Center beckoning you, it would be tempting to pass up the opportunity to investigate the eateries in here. If you do, you'll miss two gems tucked kitty-corner next to each other. **Ristorante Roma** (620 S. Rangeline Road) is a tiny and incredibly authentic Italian restaurant. Once inside, you'll feel as though you've been transported to a different place and time; a floor-to-ceiling mural of the old Italian countryside covers one full wall in the intimate dining room. Chef and owner Lucio Romani runs the line every night, preparing family recipes that he brought to Carmel from his native Italy, and makes his pastas in-house. Because the back door of Ristorante Roma peeks out onto the Monon Trail, Romani also added a gelato bar called Mamma Mia. It's the perfect spot to enjoy a creamy Italian treat in

HAMILTON COUNTY FOOD SUPERSTAR MATT FREY

Carmel native Matt Frey opened Bub's in 2003 in a quaint, Victorian-style house that has served as a private home, a car repair shop, a flower shop and a café called That One Place. Frey graduated from Carmel High School in 1989 and worked for years as food broker, so he'd been around the restaurant business for a while. He had been talking about opening a restaurant in Carmel that had some local flair and would give the ubiquitous chain restaurants a run for their money.

"I'd been looking for a location for a while when I came across the for-sale sign in the front. I knew this was the perfect location, so I jumped out of my car, called the number on the sign and then hid the sign in the snow. With the help of family and friends, Bub's was born. We really just wanted to provide an alternative to the chains, and we wanted to serve really great food made in our own kitchen with love. We started out with burgers and fries, but the menu evolved as we went along. One day, an elk farmer showed up in the kitchen. I resisted at first, but I decided to give it a try. And people really liked it.

"In 2007, we opened Bub's Café down the trail," he continued. "We serve breakfast and lunch only there, and it's usually pretty jumping. We keep ourselves pretty busy."

Frey is deeply committed to the community and serves on numerous boards, including those of the chamber of commerce and Carmel Youth Assistance.

Matt Frey. *Photo provided.*

the summer months. The proximity to the Center for the Performing Arts makes it a great place to enjoy a preshow dinner.

Just next door to Ristorante Roma, you'll find Carmel mainstay **Soho Café**. Soho is the go-to meeting place for locals and tourists alike. It features outdoor seating along the Monon Trail and a spacious seating area filled with local artists' work, mismatched furniture and a cozy fireplace. The café frequently hosts live music showcasing local musicians. Longtime Carmel resident Alan Potasnik fondly remembers when this spot was home to a steakhouse called Dunham's Prime Time Restaurant. These days, generous cups of lattes and cappuccinos are served with a smile, generally in chipped and mismatched coffee mugs, the way a real coffee shop should do it.

THE CITY CENTER

The glittering City Center is a foodie's dream. It's an island unto itself, so once you've secured a place to park in the on-site garage, plan to spend some time wandering the lovely boutiques and eateries. It's not huge, but it's packed with quality destinations and absolutely worth a stop.

The most interesting dinner spot here is **divvy**, at 71 City Center Drive. It's owned and operated by the owners of Woody's Library, Woody and Richelle Rider. It's the perfect spot for a quick bite before a performance at Carmel's spectacular Center for the Performing Arts.

While small-plate concepts are ubiquitous elsewhere, they're relatively rare in Hamilton County. However, divvy has the concept nailed with a mind-boggling assortment of creative small plates and hand-crafted cocktails. You must be at least twenty-one years old to go to divvy, so this place is for grown-up nights on the town. The spacious patio features lovely views of the Center Green, which connects the three theaters of the Center for the Performing Arts. It's a great spot for people-watching.

You could dine here every day for a month and still not cover the menu, but whatever you try, don't miss the corn crème brûlée. An absolutely addictive savory twist on the dessert version of this dish, it's slightly spicy, sweet and creamy all at the same time. The lobster quesadilla will also knock your socks off.

Right next door to divvy is **Books & Brews**. Given its swanky address, it's a little more upscale than its Fishers relative, but it still maintains that funky, feel-good vibe, and true to its name, it's loaded with books.

Just next to Books & Brews is **Eggshell Bistro**. Opened in 2011 by designer Larry Hanes, it's part restaurant, part art. The quirky atmosphere is matched by a completely unique menu. If you're in the market for scrambled eggs, bacon and a bottomless cup of coffee, you're in the wrong place. Even the most sophisticated foodies will find themselves pulling out their phones to look up ingredients in dishes such as the moulard rouge—a prosciutto-wrapped, smoked duck breast with cranberry chévre and a Luxardo-pomegranate-sorghum sauce topped with a frizzled hen's egg and

The entrance to the artsy and upscale Eggshell Bistro in Carmel's City Center. *Photo by Larry Hanes.*

served on a buckwheat, black sesame waffle. (You made that at home last week, right?) The sweet potato hash is also a knockout, studded with chorizo, gooseberries, jalapeños and scallions and topped with crème fraîche and two sous vide hen's eggs.

On the back side of the City Center is **Hubbard and Cravens** (703 Veteran's Way), established in 1991 out of a simple desire to offer fine coffee and tea in Indianapolis. Rick Hubbard and Jerry Cravens have expanded their local empire quite a bit. Their posh coffee shop and eatery in Carmel's City Center is host to many a power breakfast for Carmel's movers and shakers. The menu has grown up over the years, and this location now features a full juice and smoothie bar and a creative menu of breakfast and lunch fare that focuses heavily on locally sourced ingredients, including Trader's

HAMILTON COUNTY FOOD SUPERSTARS WOODY AND RICHELLE RIDER: WOODY'S LIBRARY AND DIVVY

Richelle and Woody Rider. *Photo provided.*

Kevin "Woody" Rider is a fixture in Carmel, and you'll often find him trekking down Main Street between his two restaurants, divvy and Woody's Library. While Woody works the front of the house, his wife, Richelle, oversees the kitchens of both as executive chef. They opened Woody's Library in 1998 and divvy in 2011.

Woody was working as a restaurant consultant when he came upon the location for Woody's Library. It was built as a Carnegie library in 1913 and functioned as such until 1970. Then, it served as Carmel's city hall from 1972 to 1989. When a new city hall was built, the city sold the old one at auction. After the building had languished for several years, the Riders saw the potential for the building to become a restaurant and began the work to restore it.

"When your restaurant is in an old building, people have an instant sense of belonging," said Woody. "That's not something you can buy. Carmel was built by Quakers, so a lot of the buildings are wood. It's not easy to find a historic brick structure around here like it is in Noblesville. But I will say there was a ton of work involved. The bookshelves that used to be built-in were laying all over the floor, and I had to figure out how they all fit together. And I think I pulled about 10,000 staples out of that floor!

"There was not much in terms of restaurants downtown when we opened," Rider continued. "The Glass Chimney was serving fine-dining cuisine on the other side of town. Other than that, most Carmel residents didn't stay in Carmel for dinner. It took us a while to draw the families in, but over the years, it's definitely evolved as a family place. You'll often find me walking around holding someone's baby so that mom and dad can both eat their dinners. We were after that small-town, comfortable feel.

"With divvy, we were looking to do the opposite. We wanted to bring a big city feel to Carmel, and the tapas phenomenon was not widely known here when we opened the doors. It's definitely a place for a sophisticated evening, and it's an adult restaurant. But I hope we're finding a way to make everyone, locals and tourists alike, happy when they're here in Carmel."

Point Creamery cheeses, Smoking Goose cured meats and Scholar's Inn baked goods. This is also not a place to expect bottomless cups of coffee and heaping piles of hash browns, but the turkey hash is delightful. It features diced breast of turkey on a bed of roasted potatoes and onion and is finished with a delicate béchamel sauce and a farm-fresh egg.

Before you leave Rangeline Road, there's one more stop to make. There's another location of the **Flying Cupcake Bakery** at 831 S. Range Line Road (get the lowdown on these lovelies from the Fishers listing). There are cupcakes. Really, really, good cupcakes. Enough said.

BEYOND THE CONFINES OF DOWNTOWN

No visit anywhere near Indianapolis is complete without a stop at a Martha Hoover restaurant. Hoover oversees an ever-expanding culinary empire, and Carmel is lucky to have not one but two of her **Café Patachou** restaurants—one in the Clay Terrace Mall, at 14390 Clay Terrace Boulevard, and the other just off Hazel Dell Parkway at 5790 E. Main Street.

Billed as a "student union for adults," the Patachou restaurants first appeared on the Indianapolis-area dining scene in 1989 and are one of the original farm-to-table concepts in Hamilton County. The Patachou restaurants are not cheap, but they're worth every penny for the fresh ingredients, which are simply prepared, and the delightful service and ambiance. It's not just locals who love it—Café Patachou has been named one of the "Top Ten Places for Breakfast in the Country" by *Bon Appétit* magazine.

If you're a fan of smoked salmon, the Ora-King sustainable smoked salmon bagel is heaven, with all the traditional garniture: tomatoes, cream cheese, red onions, capers and diced egg. The duck confit hash is also divine, and their signature tomato artichoke soup will have you wanting to return every day for the rest of your life.

Just up Hazel Dell Parkway from Café Patachou is **Pizzology Craft Pizza & Pub** (13190 Hazel Dell Parkway). Offering exceptional pizza and so much more, Pizzology is committed to utilizing local ingredients, including Smoking Goose cured meats, Tulip Tree cheeses and fresh vegetables from area farmers. Lovely starters include a crispy eggplant salad, wood-roasted mushroom risotto, steamed Prince Edward Island mussels and (in season) an asparagus and orzo salad. The house-made ricotta is finished with truffle oil, fresh oregano and sea salt and served with grilled Italian bread. The pappardelle bolognese, made with Gunthorp Farms pork braised in red wine and enveloped in a robust tomato sauce on a bed of pappardelle pasta, is a treat. And then, of course, there's pizza.

Mimi Blue Meatballs, at 12505 Old Meridian Street, is named for Mildred (Mimi) Bluestein Kosene, an elegant woman who lived her whole life in Indianapolis. It is owned and operated by her sons David and Gerry and her grandson Michael, who named the restaurant to pay homage to a woman who loved to cook and never met a stranger. The original Mimi Blue opened on Massachusetts Avenue in Indianapolis in 2014, and the Carmel location opened in 2016. The unique menu is mostly just meatballs—available in classic, turkey, veggie or beef—accompanied by a choice of sauces, including marinara, mushroom gravy, honey sriracha, barbeque and bolognese. There's a nice assortment of side dishes, as well.

Start with the truffle creamed gnocchi and follow it with the turkey meatballs topped with spicy cilantro sauce. For sides, choose the fried Brussels sprouts and creamy polenta. If you can make it to dessert, Mimi's Own banana mousse with whipped cream and vanilla wafers will take you back to your childhood.

Just north of Mimi Blue is the **Brockway Public House**. Husband-and-wife team Kevin "KP" and Lainie Paul have owned and operated the Brockway Public House in Carmel since 2008. It's a tried-and-true neighborhood Irish pub that features traditional pub fare and live music, just in case you feel like dancing a jig.

A little farther north, on the hallowed grounds where the **Glass Chimney** once welcomed the swells, is **Bru Burger** at 12901 Old Meridian Street. The spot languished for years before Indianapolis-based Cunningham Restaurant Group (CRG) snapped it up. CRG is a driving force in the Circle

HAMILTON COUNTY FOOD SUPERSTAR MARTHA HOOVER

Martha Hoover's influence is felt not just in Hamilton County but throughout central Indiana and beyond. Until the late 1980s, Hoover made her living as an attorney, but her love of good food had been cemented when she visited Paris as a teenager, and restaurants seemed to be her destiny.

Hoover's food empire continues to expand with more Patachou concepts, as well as Napolese Pizzerias, Public Greens and Petite Chou Bistro and Champagne Bar. The first Café Patachou opened in Carmel on Gray Road in 1997. That location has closed, and a newer, more spacious location opened in its place in 2017 at Hazel Dell Parkway and Main Street. Hoover is absolutely a pioneer in central Indiana's farm-to-table movement, having opened the first Patachou concept in Indianapolis in 1989.

"We have always served locally sourced, scratch-made, high quality food to our customers, and we have refused to deliver anything less. We are proud to foster true and meaningful relationships with small family farms and producers and have always done so, even before the term farm-to-table entered the foodie vernacular," said Hoover. "There is a generation of people coming of age in this area who truly care about sustainability, conscious food sourcing, and commitment to the community and are looking for restaurants with the same social consciousness. It has taken a while, but it is extremely rewarding to see."

Martha Hoover. *Photo provided.*

Hoover, along with Patachou's executive chef Tyler Herald, continues to blaze trails on the food scene here in various ways. In 2013, she formed a not-for-profit foundation to teach kids how to grow and eat healthy foods, and today, the Patachou Foundation serves nearly one thousand meals per week to food-insecure children across the Indianapolis metropolitan area.

Fortune Magazine named Hoover one of its "2017 Most Innovative Women in Food and Drink" not just for her wildly successful dining concepts and not-for-profit endeavors but also for her approach to employee engagement and retention. All employees in her restaurants have health benefits and 401(k) plans, among numerous other generous perks. Hoover was also profiled in *Vogue* in 2018 for her approach to food sustainability.

City's culinary renaissance, and Bru Burger, like all of their concepts, delivers tasty food with style and a smile. This casual, chef-driven gastropub never disappoints. While there are tons of great choices, the sriracha Caesar salad is particularly addictive, and the Spaniard burger—with arugula, Serrano ham, pickled shishito peppers, romesco sauce, manchego cheese and onion jam—is killer. Just a smidge farther north on Old Meridian, you'll find the Carmel location of **Rosie's Place** at 1111 W. Main Street. (Remember, we *told* you about those butter cookies!)

Upland Brewing Company originated in Bloomington and was founded by partners Marc Sattinger, Russ Levitt and Dean LaPlante. It now boasts locations in Indianapolis, Columbus and Carmel. **Upland Brewing Company's Carmel Tap House**, at 820 E. 116th Street, is warm and welcoming, with a spacious outdoor patio accessible from the Monon Trail. Live music is often featured on the patio in the summer months. The food is not typical bar fare; it's top-notch cuisine prepared with local ingredients and a strong focus on vegetarian dishes.

For example, the local Fischer Farms pork chop with smashed raspberry compote, accompanied by sautéed Brussels sprouts and jalapeño cornbread, is far and above anything you'd expect in a brew pub. And if you don't want pork, the macaroni and cheese—made with their signature Upland Wit beer and loads of garlic—is heaven. Their seitan tenderloin sandwich might make you forget about pork altogether.

As previously mentioned, it's hard to miss a restaurant owned by the Wolf family in Hamilton County. The Carmel **Wolfie's Northern Woods Grill**, at 1162 Keystone Way, feels like a pretty straightforward family dining spot, but the cozy private dining room, with its massive stone fireplace, will make you feel like you've teleported from Indiana to a posh ski resort in Colorado. It's gorgeous.

While most of the culinary action in Carmel happens east of Meridian, there are a few spots that are worth a drive west. **Convivio Italian**

The entrance to Bru Burger, in Carmel, which used to be the legendary Glass Chimney restaurant. *Photo provided.*

Artisan Cuisine is tucked away in a strip mall at 11529 Spring Mill Road, near the amazing **Market District** grocery store. It offers a stunning menu featuring house-made pastas and rustic Italian cuisine in a sleek, modern space.

Danny Boy Beer Works, located at 12702 Meeting House Road, is the second venture of Brockway Public House's KP and Lainie Paul in partnership with Sara and Prescott Sanders. They opened Danny Boy in 2014, realizing their dream of owning a brewery along with head brewer Dustin Brown. Danny Boy has a cool, industrial vibe and a huge outdoor patio that always feels like you're at a party at a good friend's house. They now have around ten house brews, including Training Day, an American pale ale, and, in honor of their Irish roots, Church, a sweet Irish milk stout.

The food is all served in a no-frills manner. The Texas-style brisket, locally sourced from Moody Meats in Zionsville, arrives on a wax paper–lined baking sheet with cornbread and your choice of side.

The latest addition to Ed Sahm's restaurant empire, **Sahm's Ale House at the Village of West Clay**, located at 12819 E. New Market Street, opened its doors in 2018. Ed Sahm's son Eddie and brewmaster

HAMILTON COUNTY FOOD SUPERSTAR NEAL BROWN

Chef/owner Neal Brown opened Pizzology Craft Pizza & Pub in 2009. He's widely considered to be one of the top chefs in the Midwest, having been nominated twice for the James Beard Foundation's "Best Chef in the Midwest" award. Brown operates several other restaurants in the Indianapolis area, including Libertine Liquor Bar, a trendy, craft cocktail gastropub, and Ukiyo, a hip, Japanese-inspired restaurant in the up-and-coming SoBro restaurant district in Indianapolis. Ukiyo occupies the space that once housed revered Indy chef Greg Hardesty's Recess.

"Pizzology's primary mission has always been to get folks to understand that farm-to-table food doesn't have to come in a fine dining package," said Brown. "There is a very sophisticated diner in this region, and they were not being served at the time we opened Pizzology. We want people to have access to the highest quality food they can, and we do everything we can to provide it. We still make everything in-house, including all of our cheeses. We ferment our own dough and source product from local farms that grow and raise food in a way that is environmentally sustainable.

"Since the time we opened our doors, the dining scene has certainly become more robust," he continued. "I've particularly been impressed with the growth of independent restaurateurs in the eight years we've been in business. We, along with many other locally owned independent restaurants here in Hamilton County, care about our community, and therefore, the community cares about us."

Neal Brown. *Photo provided.*

Scott Ellis are co-owners. The space was formerly occupied by a short-lived venture called the Lit Moose, and, prior to that, Neal Brown's Pizzology. The Ale House menus are a hybrid of the Sahm's and Rockstone Pizza concepts. They offer traditional comfort food, stir-fries, pastas, tacos and wood-fired pizza, so it's easy to find something for everyone. Everything on the menu pairs with beer, as well it should; Sahm's Big Lug brews rule the drink list.

7

WESTFIELD

Can't-Miss Destinations and Culinary Superstars

Westfield is a city just coming into its own. The landscape is lovely, with rolling meadows and horse farms that harken back to the earlier days of Hamilton County before the start of the development boom. It's long been an idyllic place to live, but residents have, until recently, had limited dining choices near their homes. Now, however, the game is changing.

Part of the impetus for that was the opening of the Grand Park sporting complex in 2014. It covers four hundred acres of what used to be mostly farmland and now hosts around 750,000 visitors per year. The demand for more dining options in Westfield continues to increase from visitors and locals alike, and restaurateurs are responding.

One of the coolest places to come along in Westfield is **Rail Epicurean Market** at 211 Park Street. Owned by husband-and-wife team Melanie and Toby Miles, it originally had just a simple counter with a few pastries in a case. It's now grown up into a rustic-chic eatery with a full liquor license featuring cocktails made with Bloomington-based Cardinal Spirits and great cuisine. It's tucked away off the beaten path, so you'll have to look to find it, but it's absolutely worth the effort. If the bourbon-glazed chicken and waffle is on the menu, forget your diet and go for it.

The Italian House on Park is right next door at 219 Park Street. It's owned and operated by the Wolf family, who own and operate all the Wolfie's restaurants throughout Hamilton County. Located in a converted single-family home, the dining rooms are upscale and quaint, with white linen tablecloths and fresh flowers. They make full use of the space, so you might even find yourself seated in the garage, which is much lovelier than it sounds. If you're in the mood for something more casual, the Backyard Bar is a great spot to enjoy comfy seating around a fire pit with live music.

Super Bowl Pho, at 112 E. Main Street, is a fantastic addition to the Westfield dining scene. For starters, the location is special. This spot was home to Daugherty's Coffee Shop in the 1950s and then Marlow's Café for more than forty years after that. It's newly swanky these days, with linen tablecloths and a cheery décor, serving bright, zesty Southeast Asian flavors to Hamilton County diners who appreciate authentic Vietnamese cuisine. It's family-owned and has been rated the No. 1 Vietnamese restaurant in the United States on Yelp. The huge menu offers crispy spring rolls, loads of heavenly lemongrass-laced dishes, noodles, udon and, of course, pho—the earthy, savory broth-based dish that is the hallmark of Vietnamese cuisine. Try the traditional bahn mi—a soft French roll spread with paté and topped with Vietnamese sausage, steamed pork belly, pickled vegetables and cilantro.

The **Grand Junction Brewing Company Brew Pub**, at 110 S. Union Street, is a downtown institution, but they're growing. The name harks back to the great days of the Monon and Midland Railroads that intersected in Westfield in the 1800s, with a nod to the Underground Railroad. The brewery was opened in 2014 by partners Jon Knight and Charlie Wood along with brewmaster Shawn Kessel. They specialize in European-style brews, such as the Mulligan Scottish Ale. The building that houses the brew pub is near Asa Bales Park, which is named for one of the Quakers who played a pivotal role in the Underground Railroad. Fish and chips is their signature dish—a half-pound of cod battered in their own Nut Brown Ale. Wash it down with a Hoosier Pride Cream Ale.

In 2017, the owners brought to life the **Grand Junction Brewing Company Tap Room** at 1189 E. 181st Street. The newer, three-thousand-square-foot taproom has a great, industrial vibe. It's located in a converted lumberyard near Grand Park and is welcoming to kids, dogs and cyclists.

Another incredibly cool destination here is the **Urban Vines Winery and Brewery** at 303 E. 161st Street. Serial entrepreneur and biochemist Noah Herron opened Urban Vines in 2017 after owning and operating the Urban Farmer seed company for eight years. While he's still in the seed business, he's now branched out into making both wine and beer. He also designed the Indiana-shaped labels for all the wines. The urban-rustic and intimate tasting room sits on a beautiful piece of land that is essentially in

Herron's backyard. There's abundant outdoor seating and live music most every weekend. If you get hungry from all those wine samplings, there are lovely charcuterie plates, featuring Smoking Goose and other local producers, on which to nosh.

Right next door to Grand Junction Brew Pub is **Jan's Village Pizza** at 108 S. Union Street. Other than Bernie Pickett's notorious ghost, Jan's is known for great pizza. Husband-and-wife team Steve and Jan Miller have built a steady business for nearly twenty years. The dough is made in-house and comes out perfectly thin and crispy. They use good ingredients, such as fresh basil, and offer creative house pies like the Mediterranean, which is topped with spinach, feta, basil, chicken, banana peppers and bacon. A nice selection of starters, salads, sandwiches and pasta rounds out the menu.

Erika's Place, at 102 S. Union Street, is along this stretch as well. If you love local diners and dives, Erika's Place is your spot. It's clean and cheerfully painted, but it's as down to earth as you can get. The service is no-nonsense, bordering on brusque—but then again, they're really busy. It's always packed, so go early or plan to be patient. A fully stocked toy chest will keep the kids busy while you wait. Although no research has been done to back up this claim, it may very well be the only restaurant in Hamilton County that serves fried bologna. If you're looking for Indiana chicken and noodles outside of Amish country, this is the place to go. It's also one of just a few places where one can find liver and onions these days. Breakfast is available all day.

Just down Main Street, you'll find yet another Hamilton County **Wolfie's Northern Woods Grill**. It's a great spot for late-night dining in a town that closes up shop pretty early.

Tucked in a strip mall at 14655 Gray Road is a conundrum of a restaurant called **The Local**. You'd never find it if you weren't looking for it. The ambiance, with bright overhead lights, concrete floors and hardwood booths, suggests that this is just another burger joint. But while there are certainly burgers to be had, the "market specials" section of the menu tells a very different tale. Here, you'll find delightful offerings such as crispy duck leg confit on a bed of squash and pickled radish, fried shishito peppers with green tomatoes and lemon-sesame vinaigrette or a lovely shrimp piccata on linguini with a silky lemon, caper, garlic and butter sauce. It's hands-down one of the best restaurants in Hamilton County.

When it comes to sourcing locally, they live up to their name. A large chalkboard near the back lists every local farmer and grower featured on the

HAMILTON COUNTY FOOD SUPERSTAR CRAIG BAKER

Craig Baker grew up in Pennsylvania and found his culinary footing in Portland, Oregon. Cooking in the Pacific Northwest taught him to seek out and respect what was local and extraordinarily fresh. After life brought him to the Indianapolis area in the early 2000s, he was surprised to find a disconnect between what local farmers were growing and what was showing up on local restaurants' plates. While a few restaurants in downtown Indianapolis were dabbling in fledgling farm-to-table concepts, no one in Hamilton County was, and the concept for The Local was born. Baker, along with business partner Derek Means, found the location just off 146th Street and opened the doors in February 2011.

"Our goal was to create a farm-to-table concept that elevated the cuisine but was still family friendly," Baker said. "We expected a slow start. But three months after we opened, we made the *Indianapolis Monthly* list of Top 25 Best New Restaurants. We got clobbered then, and it really hasn't let up much since. When we first opened, we were making our own tater tots. That's no longer possible, given that we now serve around 24,000 pounds of them a year."

The Local currently buys all their beef from the Indiana Beef Co-op, which represents around nine ranches in central and southern Indiana. Their duck comes from Maple Leaf Farms in Leesburg, Indiana. Given that Baker grew up in Pennsylvania, he felt a pretty strong affinity to Heinz ketchup. But after taking a fair amount of ribbing, he's switched to Red Gold and also uses their canned tomato products. Baker is a history buff and loves to experiment with cooking techniques from the days before refrigeration was commonplace. As a result, you'll

Craig Baker. *Photo provided.*

find smoked, pickled and cured foods on the menu as he dabbles. Baker has also created menus for the historical Hearthside Suppers at Conner Prairie in Fishers.

Author's Note: Baker has since left The Local. However, his contributions to the early farm-to-table movement in Hamilton County are undeniable, and he'll always be a Hamilton County Food Superstar.

menu that week. You'll find it packed full of families most every night of the week. The kitchen staff takes pride in being able to accommodate most any dietary restriction, and nut- and gluten-free items are clearly noted on the menu. The bar offers a great selection of martinis and specialty cocktails (try the blackberry lemonade!) as well as local brews and a sturdy little wine list.

If it's barbeque you're after, **Big Hoffa's Barbeque**, at 800 E. Main Street, is your spot. California native Adam Hoffman (Big Hoffa) opened his tiny barbeque spot in a vacant coffee shop space in 2003. Hoffman cooks from his family's recipes, making salad dressings, sides, sauces and desserts from scratch daily. They whip up four hundred gallons of barbeque sauce every week and slow-smoke over ten thousand pounds of meat every month. Hoffman has planted a garden in front of the restaurant and grows fresh vegetables for use in the restaurant in season.

While you can't go wrong with a classic rack of ribs, if you're feeling adventurous, try the Saigon—it's pulled pork with spicy mayo, pickled onions, carrots and radishes, finished with cilantro and jalapeño.

John Perazzo closed his original **J. Razzo's**, located in Carmel, in 2018. Thus, his Westfield location, which he opened in 2013, is called **J. Razzo's 2**. It's located at 3150 E. State Road 32. They make all their sauces and salad dressings from scratch daily, as well as some of their breads and pastas. Gluten-free pasta is also an option. They offer a fantastic and reasonably priced wine list and a full bar. If you're torn between all the delectable choices, the gnocchi with spicy tomato cream, bacon and calabrese peppers is amazing, as are the Italian sausage–stuffed dates with romesco sauce. Don't leave without trying the risotto balls, which are made of delectable deep-fried risotto and stuffed with mozzarella and sweet peas.

To start or finish your Westfield culinary adventure on a sweet note, don't miss **Titus Bakery at Monon Marketplace** at 17471 Wheeler Road. This family-owned bakery has been open since the 1950s and is on its third generation of bakers. Originally owned by Bill Titus, the business was taken over by his daughter Terry in 2012. She has since expanded the business from a simple pastry shop into a café offering sandwiches made from Boar's Head lunch meat as well as a signature line of coffees and popcorn. But pastries still rule here, ranging from a staggering array of doughnut flavors to cakes, cookies, pies, turnovers, muffins, eclairs and cannoli. They're famous for the Pershing, which is a heavenly cinnamon-maple pastry doughnut, and their award-winning maple bacon doughnut is lovely, too. There are freshly baked treats for your canine friends as well.

8

OTHER HAMILTON COUNTY COMMUNITIES AND BEYOND

Can't-Miss Destinations and Culinary Superstars

While Noblesville, Carmel, Fishers and Westfield pack a lot of culinary action into more densely populated areas, there are some shining stars in the smaller Hamilton County communities of Cicero, Sheridan, Arcadia and Atlanta that should not be missed, and a few that are just outside of Hamilton County's borders but are too good to leave out.

CICERO

10 West, the hip oasis that anchors the intersection of Peru (IN 19) and Jackson Streets in Cicero's otherwise relatively sleepy downtown, is absolutely worth seeking out. Chef Bill Wampler oversees the kitchen, while Lisa Wampler runs the dining room. It's owned by Brett Morrow. Live music is often featured in the downstairs bar and dining area, which feels like a party in your coolest friend's basement.

The twisted taco section of the menu features unique taco fillings, including plum pork with ginger slaw and scallions and peanut chicken—tender chicken thighs marinated in soy and ginger topped with pickled red onion and cilantro. If you're in the mood for a great steak, you'll find it here.

Vestiges of the old **Anvil Inn** and the original character of the building's long history remain at **Big Dog's Smokehouse** at 29 E. Jackson Street. Big Dog's is owned and operated by husband-and-wife team Chris and Cheryl Faulkner (with a little help from their five kids). While the atmosphere here is much more laid back than that of their esteemed predecessor, the Faulkners cut no corners—sauces, rubs and desserts are all made in-house, and they're always smoking something new. The brisket is killer here—melt-in-your-mouth tender. Try it with the Carolina sauce—a nontraditional, piquant mustard vinegar. You absolutely must save room for dessert. The St. Louis gooey butter cake is made from scratch daily from Cheryl's grandmother's recipe.

DeLullo's Trattoria, at 230 W. Jackson Street, is owned by Hamilton County native Kay DeLullo, who is also the chef. She's all about fresh and local ingredients. She recently moved the restaurant from Atlanta to neighboring Cicero, where it is now located in a cute converted house. They grow a good portion of their own produce and make their own maple syrup and ice cream. The menu offers pizza, enormous oven-baked hoagies and a "pasta by you" section in which you choose the type of pasta, the sauce and the toppings. There are specialty pastas as well. You really have to save room for dessert and try the bomba exotic; it's mango, passionfruit and raspberry sorbetto encased in a white-chocolate shell.

If you want to go where the locals go, check out **Cicero Coffee Company** at 150 S. Peru Street. It's the best place in tiny Cicero for coffee, company and sustenance. They bake from scratch and specialize in vegetarian, vegan and gluten-free items. There's even live music on weekends. For a soul-satisfying lunch, try the chicken velvet soup. For dessert, the locals rave about the buckeye pie.

Also in Cicero, you'll find second locations of Westfield's popular **Erika's Place**, at 40 W. Jackson Street, and **Titus Bakery**, at 820 W. South Street.

SHERIDAN

The Blackhawk Winery and Vineyard, at 28153 Ditch Road, is owned by husband and wife John and Deb Miller. The Millers own a large piece of land in Sheridan, and in 2011, they decided that the five-acre soybean field on their land would be better served growing grapes. They converted the pole barn into a combination production facility and tasting room. In 2016, they purchased adjacent land and expanded their vineyards. In addition to offering wine, trivia nights, live music and murder mystery events add to the fun. Their semi-dry Cayuga White is lovely; fruit-forward with a crisp finish, it's a perfect summer sipping wine. And in the colder months, the rich and round Chambourcin red will warm your bones. If the prospect of some great wine isn't enough to draw you in, there's a herd of adorable "baby doll" sheep on the property that are tasked with weed control in the vineyards. They're worth a trip all on their own.

If you happen to have a hankering for some apples, **Stuckey Farm Market**, at 19975 Hamilton Boone Road, is your place. The sprawling farm boasts over four thousand trees producing twenty-seven varieties of apples that you can pick yourself. You could spend an entire day here taking a wagon ride through the orchard, watching the cider press in action, having a picnic or browsing the market. On weekends in the fall, they have themed "Harvest Weekend" events and fifteen acres of pumpkin patch.

Also in Sheridan, you'll find another outpost of **Jan's Village Pizza** at 200 S. Main Street. It's just as good as the one in Westfield, but as far as we know, this one's not haunted.

ARCADIA

Family-owned by Bill and Judy Wilson for over forty years, the **Wilson Farm Market** started out as a place where passersby could get fresh eggs out of an old refrigerator on the honor system and leave their money in a muffin tin. It's since grown to become a full-fledged market (they call it a "general store") that has a deli counter and sells fruits and vegetables, homemade baked goods, Amish cheese, all-natural Yoder's meats from Shipshewana, house-made fudge and fried chicken. In the spring, this is a place where you could get your hands on some locally foraged morel mushrooms. In the summer months, you'll find some of the best Indiana sweet corn in the state.

ATLANTA

It's probably safe to assume that you've never dined inside a tractor dealership. Well, if you have ten dollars in your pocket and a desire to have breakfast or lunch surrounded by tractors, combines and other lawn equipment, you can certainly fill your belly at the **Combine Café** in the Reynolds Farm Equipment store at 1451 E. 276th Street. The breakfast menu offers mostly standard fare, but you might be surprised to find a BLT made with applewood-smoked bacon on toasted sourdough and fig balsamic mayo in the middle of a field surrounded by green and yellow farm equipment. Only in Indiana.

Speaking of things that are quintessentially Indiana, let's talk about pie. If you're going to get serious about it, you must visit **Lisa's Pie Shop** at 5995 S U.S. Highway 31. It's nestled between acres of farm fields on this long stretch of highway and is a perfect place to jump out of the car, stretch your legs and—of course—eat some pie! Lisa's offers a dazzling array of flavors; in addition to traditional fruit pies like apple and cherry, seasonal flavors include black raspberry, strawberry-rhubarb and peach. There is also an amazing selection of cream pies (including Indiana's signature sugar cream), several specialty pies, cookies, breads and quiche. If you're on the road and want to take the taste of Lisa's with you over a long distance, you can grab an assortment of their unique pies-in-a-jar to enjoy later.

JUST BEYOND

At first pass, Fortville's Main Street looks like just about any other Main Street in Smalltown, USA. But nestled amongst the quaint, historic buildings on Fortville's Main Street that house pizza joints, antique shops and insurance agencies, you'll find two foodie havens that rival anything the big city has to offer: **Foxgardin Kitchen and Ale**, at 215 S. Main Street, and **Taxman Brewing Company**, at 29 S. Main Street.

Foxgardin Kitchen and Ale is the perfect combination of a cozy, local dive bar and a hip, urban-chic, twenty-one-and-over eatery. The staff is friendly, and the handcrafted drinks are reasonably priced. The menu changes with the seasons and takes a few crazy twists and turns—the "unconventional chili" is topped with provolone and peanut butter—but the entrée selections are solid, and the option of having a six-, eight- or ten-ounce filet is a nice touch. It might look like the kind of place where you should stick with a burger, but dishes like the seared scallops, with orange beurre blanc accompanied by mashed potatoes and asparagus, are divine. Great news came for the Fishers family foodie scene when Foxgardin opened **Foxgardin Family Kitchen at Geist**, located at 10410 Olio Road.

Just down the street from Foxgardin Kitchen and Ale, Taxman Brewing Company is just straight-up cool. Husband-and-wife team Leah and Nathan Huelsebusch, along with partners Matt Rogers and Brian Fisk, opened Taxman's second location in Fortville in 2017. The original location is south of Indianapolis in Bargersville. Because the Huelsebusches are Belgian,

Foxgardin Kitchen and Ale in Fortville. *Photo by author.*

waffles are a thing here, as are Belgian beers. But other than the pearl sugar they import to make their signature Liege waffles, those Belgian items are made with locally sourced ingredients. The menu is quirky and creative. The food doesn't ever come quickly, but it's worth the wait.

Obviously, the Belgian frites are a must-have, as are the Liege waffles, which are offered in a variety of preparations. If you're feeling adventurous, try the Rockefeller, which comes with fried oysters, spinach pesto, blue cheese, cocktail sauce and bacon. If you're not, go for the more traditional

Cordon Bleu. There are nearly twenty brews to choose from. In winter weather, warm your bones with Death and Taxes, their imperial stout. In the summer, opt for the light and refreshing Wit-held Belgian wit.

In McCordsville, CEO, head brewer and Indiana native Eilise Lane rounded up a group of primarily female investors and opened **Scarlet Lane Brewing Company** at 7724 Depot Street in 2014. Her brews are inspired by her time in Oregon, and she brews Indiana beer with a northwestern style. The dramatic labels for the company's beers are created by Oregon tattoo artist Ian McVay. The taphouse is a converted barn with reclaimed furniture and bare-bones décor. There's ample outdoor seating, along with fire pits to warm your toes. The only food available for purchase is Broad Ripple Chips, but you can bring your own food if you're in need of sustenance to go with your brews. Live music and other special events add to the fun. The Dorian Espresso Stout is one of their originals. It's a creamy porter with loads of coffee, chocolate and malt flavors that's as much dessert as it is beverage.

You'll think your GPS has betrayed you as you navigate your way to the legendary **Bonge's Tavern** at 9830 West, 280 North in Perkinsville. But when you pull up in front of the bright red old general store and see the parking lot packed with cars, you'll know you've arrived someplace special. In the summer months, unless you arrive the minute the doors open, be prepared to wait. And what waiting means for most folks here is a cooler packed with liquid refreshment to sustain them until their tables are ready, along with a variety of snacks and treats. Tailgating at Bonge's is simply part of the experience, and it's enough of a scene that a security guard is employed on the weekends to keep the natives in check.

The two-story wooden house was built in 1847 and was originally a general store owned by a man named A.J. Applegate. In 1946, Charles Bonge turned the space into a tavern and ran it as such until his passing in 1989. The building was then purchased by grocery titan Don Kroger, who renovated it and converted it into a restaurant. Tony Huelster came on board as executive chef, and in 1999, he and his wife, Andrea, bought the restaurant from Kroger. Other than being forced to close for four months in 2000 due to a fire caused by a lightning strike, they've been packing patrons into the seventy-seat dining room ever since.

The menu is on a chalkboard over the bar, and the tables are covered in vinyl tablecloths, but the food speaks for itself. Many celebrities and sports personalities are fans of Bonge's, including David Letterman, Peyton Manning, A.J. Foyt, the Andretti family and Reggie Miller, so don't be

HAMILTON COUNTY FOOD SUPERSTAR TONY HUELSTER

Tony Huelster. *Photo by author.*

Bonge's Tavern chef and owner Tony Huelster is a direct descendant of the legendary Dieter Puska of Carmel's Glass Chimney. He came up through the ranks in the esteemed kitchen, starting as a pantry cook in 1980 and working his way up to chef de cuisine. He worked under Puska's tutelage until 1993, absorbing all of the classical French techniques that the demanding Puska had to teach him. Those techniques are reflected in his cooking today, even though the casual, roadhouse atmosphere of Bonge's Tavern is a far cry from the hushed environs and exacting service of the Glass Chimney.

Huelster fondly recalls his days at the Glass Chimney. "It took me five weeks to wear Dieter down. I didn't want to work anywhere else. I guess he just got tired of me beating on the door and finally hired me. I couldn't do what I do today if it weren't for Chef Puska," he said. "It was the best experience of my life. No corners were ever cut in that kitchen, and I don't cut any corners today."

While Huelster's techniques might be rooted in classical European traditions, his approach to food and style of service at Bonge's Tavern has loosened up quite a bit over the years, and he doesn't take himself too seriously. "I'm not out to make a piece of art on the plate. I'm not trying to be Picasso," he said. "Sure, I want it to look good, but most importantly, I want people to leave with a full belly and tell their friends that they had a really great meal here."

Huelster's face lights up like a kid at Christmas when he talks about fresh seafood. He's sourcing it from Florida, Alaska and everywhere in between, and he's got a source for morel mushrooms on the West Coast. He's passionate about finding the absolute best ingredients he can get his hands on, and then, in his words, "not screwing them up."

His daughter Ingrid now works on the line with him, and he taught her the same way that Puska taught him. He leads his small staff by example and hasn't hired a new server in twelve years. He jokes that one of the servers "came with the building." When you dine at Bonge's, you'll most likely see Huelster in the dining area chatting with regulars and working the room.

surprised to find yourself elbow-to-elbow with them in the tiny dining room. Reservations are only taken for parties of ten or more, and diners must be at least eighteen years old.

While there is typically a steak and some version of pork available, fish is the way to go. Huelster smokes his own salmon over applewood chips from his own apple trees, and it's amazing. Huelster prides himself on finding the absolute freshest fish available, so try any fish dish that's on the board. You may also find quail or Maple Leaf Farms duck breast on the menu. After one visit, you'll be hopelessly addicted to the jalapeño-cornbread muffins that accompany every meal. And you'll be stuffed, but you've got to have at least one bite of the sugar cream cake with warm blueberry compote.

9

A FOODIE'S PERFECT WEEKEND IN HAMILTON COUNTY (WITH AND WITHOUT KIDS)

Hamilton County boasts such a diverse and bountiful food scene, it's difficult to pare down a list to what can realistically be visited (and eaten!) in one forty-eight-hour period. Certainly, some really fantastic places won't make the cut, but this list is intended to feature a sampling of cuisines and places that are unique to Hamilton County. There's a bit of history, some walking and—since Hamilton County covers over four hundred square miles—obviously, some driving. Since a person can't eat all day long, no matter how devoted they are to that cause, it offers some sightseeing and shopping options, too. Be sure to pack a cooler in your car, as you'll definitely want to bring some treats home with you.

YOUR FOODIE HEADQUARTERS: THE PRAIRIE GUEST HOUSE

Centrally located in Fishers, the **Prairie Guest House** makes a great home base for your stay in Hamilton County. It's owned and operated by husband and wife John and Karen Newton and is housed in two historic buildings at 13805 Allisonville Road, directly across the street from the Conner Prairie interactive history center. The guest house offers nine individually decorated rooms, and it's one of the few non-chain options for lodging in Hamilton County. The guest house offers a lovely breakfast included with the room rates, but you might opt out of that in order to visit some of the stellar restaurants listed in this chapter.

Top: The historic Prairie Guest House in Fishers. *Photo provided.*

Bottom: The intimate dining room—with the original L.S. Ayres boardroom table—at the Prairie Guest House in Fishers. *Photo provided.*

The Prairie Guest House also has an interesting history. In 1852, one of the first attorneys in Hamilton County, a gentleman named Fabious Finch (who would later become William Conner's brother-in-law) built the brick Gothic-style farmhouse. Over the years, the property saw various owners, including Fabious's son, John Finch. The land was farmed by several families, and its last known agricultural use was as a horse farm. The Morehouse family lived there until they sold the property to Sue Muller and Ann Irwin in the late 1980s. Muller and Irwin transitioned the now two-and-a-half-acre plot into a bed-and-breakfast, welcoming the first guests of the Frederick Talbott Inn in the early 1990s. They sold the inn to Ed and Nancy Cohee in 2007. However, the business did not flourish during that time, and the inn closed its doors and languished, empty, until the Newtons bought it, rehabbed it and reopened it as the Prairie Guest House in February 2013. They converted one of the small outbuildings on the property into a yoga studio, and the inn offers yoga classes and retreats to guests and locals. The marvelous, whitewashed horse barn still stands on the property.

CONNER PRAIRIE INTERACTIVE HISTORY MUSEUM

If you've got the kids with you on your foodie weekend, a stop at the **Conner Prairie Interactive History Museum** is a must. Hamilton County history buffs will be excited to tour the famous William Conner's house, which is carefully preserved and open for touring from April through October. The 1836 Prairietown experience will appeal to historians, and the entire family can enjoy a ride in the iconic balloon.

In the summer months, pack a picnic from one of the many wonderful local restaurants and gourmet food shops and listen to the Indianapolis Symphony Orchestra under the stars at Symphony on the Prairie. If you're very lucky (or if you plan well), you might be able to attend a Prairie Plates event, at which some of the top chefs of the region create a unique menu around local food and artisan cocktails to offer a one-of-a-kind dining experience.

In the fall, a visit to the Apple Store is a must, and you might also try to catch the Halloween festival, complete with a corn maze, a haunted hayride and the nighttime ride of the Headless Horseman.

The "Follow the North Star" experience is a participatory theatrical presentation that takes the audience through the life of African Americans in

A hearthside supper at Conner Prairie in Fishers. *Photo provided.*

pre–Civil War Indiana and explores the inner workings of the Underground Railroad; it's presented in April and November.

SATURDAY

No visit to Hamilton County would be complete without breakfast at **Rosie's Place** in Noblesville. Get there as early as you can—they open at 8:00 a.m. and fill up quickly. After your breakfast, be prepared to fill your car with goodies for the ride home. You'll want at least a dozen ooey-gooey butter cookies. You might also want to grab a menu for future reference, as you'll undoubtedly be wanting to order online after you get home.

After breakfast, take a leisurely stroll around the Noblesville square, and if the doors of the **Hamilton County Historical Society** in the "old sheriff's house" happen to be open, go inside and check it out. There are a ton of cool historical photos and memorabilia. The building itself is worth experiencing.

If you visit during the summer, you'll find a bountiful farmer's market on Main Street. To walk off some of your breakfast, take a stroll down Eighth Street to the **Nickel Plate Arts** campus, which contains two historic buildings—the Judge Stone House and the Stephenson House, both built in the 1800s. There are revolving exhibits featuring the work of local artists, and there are eight artists' studios on site. Of particular note is the studio of artist Rodney Reveal. His work includes many paintings of historical Hamilton County buildings and famous restaurants and is featured in this book.

If you delight in otherworldly experiences, check out the **Historic Hamilton County Ghost Walks and Tours** offered by Michael and Nicole Kobrowski.

Next, head to Carmel. For lunch, grab a burger at **Bub's Burgers and Ice Cream**. If weather permits, eat al fresco and watch the endless parade of runners, walkers, dogs and strollers go by on the **Monon Trail**. If you're in the mood for some serious shopping, you can drive north to the lovely outdoor **Clay Terrace Mall**, but you can easily while away the afternoon in the adorable, locally owned boutiques in downtown Carmel.

In the afternoon, park your car anywhere on Main Street in the **Arts and Design District**. Bring your checkbook, because you'll certainly want to purchase some artwork from one of the nine locally owned art galleries. Make sure you pop into **Joe's Butcher Shop** for some local flavor. While you're strolling the streets of the Arts and Design District, you probably won't be able to resist the selfie opportunities provided by the lifelike statues, created by artist Seward Johnson, that adorn the streets. (For example, the friendly policeman assisting pedestrians in front of Bub's and the well-kept lady with a bagful of groceries in front of Joe's; there are many more.) There are numerous festivals held throughout the year, such as **Artomobilia** in August or the **Second Saturdays Gallery Walks**.

When you're ready for an afternoon pick-me-up, a stop for a glass of wine at **Peace Water Winery** is a must. The urban-chic, funky décor is worth a stop in and of itself, and the chandelier in the entryway will knock your socks off. The wine is pretty tasty, too. If you're traveling with children, substitute the wine with a delightful afternoon high tea at **Tina's Traditional English Tea Room** instead.

For dinner, if you're without kids, **divvy** is a must. The menu is incredibly diverse and creative, and the small-plates concept means that you'll get to try lots of different things. There's a huge outdoor dining space with oversized heaters, so if the weather permits, sit outside to dine with fabulous views of the stunning **Center for the Performing Arts** campus and green. divvy also features an innovative cocktail list with seasonal ingredients that are available in carafes in the spirit of sharing.

Carmel's Artomobilia, a car enthusiast's dream, happens each year in August. *Courtesy of the City of Carmel.*

If you're traveling with children, consider either **Woody's Library** or **Bazbeaux Pizza**.

Prior to your visit, check the schedule at the world-class Center for the Performing Arts. You may find a touring performance at the **Palladium** or a local production from one of the two stellar local theater groups in residence there: the equity group **Actors Theatre of Indiana** or the **Civic Theatre**. In the summer months, **Conner Prairie** offers **"Symphony on the Prairie"**—a marvelous way to spend an evening listening to the **Indianapolis Symphony Orchestra** on the lawn under the stars.

If you're traveling with children and are looking for an alternative to art galleries in the afternoon, especially in the fall, take a drive up State Road 37 and visit **Russell Farms Pumpkin Patch** instead. It's a lovely autumn outdoor adventure.

SUNDAY

For a very grown-up breakfast, head back to Carmel's City Center to **Eggshell Bistro**. If you've got kiddos along, you might opt to enjoy breakfast at the **Prairie Guest House** and then head across the street to **Conner Prairie**.

For lunch on Sunday, **The Local** in Westfield is not to be missed by kids and adults alike.

There are some amazing craft brews being produced in Hamilton County. Beer-lovers (even those with kids in tow) should consider several stops: In Fishers or Carmel, **Books & Brews** is a great way to while away a rainy Sunday. It has a reading room for the kids to putter in while mom and dad sip a pint or grab a growler in the tasting room. Also in Fishers, **Four Day Ray**, situated in the burgeoning **Fishers Town Center** on 116th Street, is kid-friendly in the dining area and has some stellar local brews.

After brunch on Sunday, you'll find that many independently owned restaurants are closed while the owners take time to be with their families. Plan ahead for this by packing a great picnic for the afternoon and heading out into one of Hamilton County's forty amazing parks and walking trails or explore the **Monon Trail**, which takes you through Hamilton County and continues through Indianapolis.

However, in the winter months, bring along your ice skates and your appetites, as the **Christkindlmarkt** in Carmel is a seasonal delight. The Christkindlmarkt features around forty vendors offering artisan craft gift items, making it perfect for holiday shopping accompanied by a nosh and cup of holiday cheer. If the kids are along and it happens to be Christmastime, you'll absolutely want to take the **Holiday Trolley** to visit Santa.

10
SUMMARY

From the days of gin joints and Prohibition through the invasion of chain restaurants and fast-food joints to the locavore movement of today, the independent restaurateur has prevailed in Hamilton County. The county now boasts a population of over 316,000 and features more than one hundred independently owned restaurants, cafés, coffee shops and artisan food markets. That number continues to grow as the population and the demand for unique menus and locally sourced food burgeons.

Hamilton County, as well as the surrounding areas of Indianapolis and the rest of central Indiana, has become a culinary force to be reckoned with and is worth a visit for any foodie who enjoys diving into a region and savoring the best that the local farms and fields have to offer. While you might be hard-pressed to find good corn pone on a menu today, a person who is so inclined can still find a whopper of a pork tenderloin sandwich, juicy fried chicken nestled on a plate of mashed potatoes and gravy, sweet corn in nearly any incarnation and sugar cream pie. But that same person can also find crispy duck wings on a bed of kimchee, a locally raised Angus beef tenderloin filet topped with locally foraged morel mushrooms swimming in garlic and butter or a hand-pressed cappuccino with a delicate, flaky, freshly baked scone. Hamilton County food has indeed come a long way.

While the chain restaurants remain (and probably always will), residents of these communities continue to show a commitment to dining local and supporting area farmers and food artisans. Unique food establishments test the waters and push the boundaries of the local food scene. Some thrive, and, sadly, some perish—either because they were ahead of their time or simply were undercapitalized from the start. But, happily, that fact doesn't deter other dreamers from taking the plunge.

This book merely scratches the surface of the robust dining scene and history of Hamilton County and the communities that surround it. It's a sobering but certainly possible fact that by the time this book appears on the shelves, some of the wonderful restaurants listed here may have closed their doors. But that's the ebb and flow of the hospitality business, and it will always be so. Whether or not the physical restaurant remains, the memories that those hardworking entrepreneurs helped to create with their patrons will last a lifetime. And in this new era of celebrating restaurants, chefs and the people who devote their lives to the business, perhaps those stories will be better chronicled for future generations. They most certainly should be. Restaurants have such a deep connection in a community, and it's important for their stories and histories to be preserved. (In today's era of Instagram and restaurant selfies, the works of art that chefs and devoted line cooks put on plates every day will almost surely be recorded for future generations to admire.)

To those of you whose restaurants, whether from days gone by or still thriving today, are featured in this book, thank you for sharing your stories, time, talents and lives with us. To those of you whose restaurants were not included, be assured that it was not because your work has gone unnoticed but simply because there are only so many pages to be filled and so many marvelous places with which to fill them. Lastly, to those of you whose restaurants have debuted on the Hamilton County restaurant scene in the time it took to publish this book, welcome. You've joined an elite group of marvelously spirited and gloriously talented folks who will embrace your contributions.

Cheers.

Appendix A

MADE IN INDIANA

A Short List of Local Growers, Food Artisans and Farmer's Markets in Hamilton County and Beyond

Throughout the book, numerous references have been made to locally sourced ingredients and products. Here's a list of some amazing Indiana growers and artisans who are either based in the greater Indianapolis area or whose products you will find frequently featured on Hamilton County menus and at local farmer's markets. There are a few food artisans here who don't sell to restaurants but can be found online and are absolutely worth seeking out. These folks, especially the farmers, are not in it to get rich (although a few of them have, happily, done pretty well). They work hard and contribute a great deal to the rich Indiana food scene in Hamilton County and beyond. This list is not all-encompassing—there are many others who are not listed here.

For great Indiana gift baskets, check out **A Taste of Indiana** online or in their Indianapolis-based storefront on Binford Boulevard.

ARTISAN FOOD PRODUCERS

Amazing Potato Chip and Popcorn Company: Indianapolis. Owner: Larry Carman

Amelia's Bakery: Indianapolis. Owner: Charlie McIntosh

B Happy Peanut Butter: Zionsville. Owners: The Weed family

Broad Ripple Chip Company: Indianapolis. Owner: Mark McSweeney

Caprini Creamery: Spiceland. Owner: Kristy Kikly
Chocolate for the Spirit: Indianapolis. Owners: Julie and Dale Bolejack
Four Birds Bakery: Indianapolis. Owner: Nicole Ankney
Heavenly Sweets: Noblesville. Owner: Tanya Marshall
Hoosier Momma Cocktail Mixers: Zionsville. Owners: KC Cranfill and Katherine Hill
Indiana Pickle Company: Indianapolis. Owner: Robert Carmack
Just Pop In Popcorn: Indianapolis. Owners: Carly Swift and Mandy Selke
Les Parisiens Patisseries: Carmel. Owner: Gilbert Serrat
Lick Ice Cream: Indianapolis. Owners: Meredith Kong and Kelly Ryan
My Pretty Little Pretzel: Carmel. Owner: Kate Gilbert
Native Bread: Indianapolis. Owner: Hayley McGinley
Pots & Pans Pie Company: Carmel. Owner: Clarissa Morley
Revival Food Co.: Indianapolis. Owner: Rachel Klein
Smoking Goose: Indianapolis. Owner: Chris Eley
Trader's Point Creamery: Zionsville. Owner: the Kunz family
Tulip Tree Creamery: Zionsville. Owner: Laura Davenport
Xchocol'Art: Carmel. Owner: Joann Hofer

FARMERS AND FARMER'S MARKETS

Annabelle's Garden: Indianapolis. Owner: Josh Horrigan
Balanced Harvest Farms: Needham. Owner: Todd Jameson
Broad Ripple Farmer's Market: Indianapolis
Carmel Farmer's Market: Carmel
Cicero Farmer's Market: Cicero
Circle City Farm: Indianapolis. Owner: John Whitesel
Earthly Delights: Carmel. Owner: Liz Chapman
Fields Farm Fresh Produce: Westfield. Owner: Rodney Fields
Fischer Farms: Jasper. Owners: Dave and Diana Fischer
Fishers Farmer's Market: Fishers
Full Hand Farm: Noblesville. Owner: Genesis McKiernan-Allen
Garcia's Gardens: Indianapolis. Owner: Daniel Garcia
Gatewoods Vegetable Farm: Noblesville. Owner: Bill Gatewood
Greenberry Farms: Whitestown. Owner: Sean Green
Gunthorp Farms: LaGrange. Owner: Greg Gunthorp
Maple Leaf Duck: Leesburg. Owners: Terry, John and Scott Tucker

My Dad's Sweet Corn: Carmel. Owner: Jennifer Baird
Noblesville Farmer's Market: Noblesville
Phelps Family Farm: Ladoga. Owner: Joe Phelps
Saxony Farmer's Market: Fishers
Shamrock Farm: Arlington. Owner: Eric Murphy
Spencer Farm: Noblesville. Owners: Kyle and Lori Spencer
St. Adrian Meats and Sausage: Lebanon. Owners: Ryan and Amelia West
Steve Zeller's Fresh Market: Noblesville. Owner: Steve Zeller
Traggesser Farm: Tipton. Owner: Chris Traggesser
Wild's Apple Farm: Zionsville. Owner: David Boots

Appendix B

HAMILTON COUNTY MAP

Hamilton County map. *Courtesy of Hamilton County Tourism.*

Appendix C

HAMILTON COUNTY FOOD ESTABLISHMENTS LISTED BY CITY

Carmel
Bazbeaux Pizza
Blu Moon Café
Books & Brews
Brockway Public House
Bru Burger
Bub's Burgers and Ice Cream
Bub's Café
Café Patachou
Convivio Italian Artisan Cuisine
Danny Boy Beer Works
divvy
Eggshell Bistro
Flying Cupcake Bakery
Hubbard and Cravens
Joe's Butcher Shop
Joe's Next Door Café
Main Street Poké
Mimi Blue Meatballs
Mudbugs Cajun Café
Peace Water Winery
Pizzology Craft Pizza & Pub
Ristorante Roma
Rosie's Place

Sahm's Ale House at the Village of West Clay
Soho Café
Tina's Traditional English Tea Room
Upland Brewing Company's Carmel Tap House
Wolfie's Northern Woods Grill
Woody's Library

Fishers
Books & Brews
Café Korea
Flying Cupcake Bakery
Four Day Ray
Foxgardin Family Kitchen
Harmony Winery
Main Street Poké
MashCraft Brewery
Nickel Plate Bar and Grill
Peterson's
Pure Eatery
Redemption Alewerks
Sahm's Restaurant and Pub
St. Yared Ethiopian Cuisine and Coffeehaus
Thai Kitchen
The Roost
The Yard Culinary District
Wild Ginger
Wolfie's at Geist
Wolfie's Northern Woods Grill
Wooden Bear Brewing at Geist

Noblesville
Asian Grill
Barley Island Brewery
Broccoli Bill's Fresh Produce and Specialty Grocery
Caplinger's Fresh Catch
Courtney's Kitchen
Deer Creek Brewery
Matteo's Ristorante Italiano
Michaelangelo's Italian Bistro

Noble Coffee and Tea Company
Rosie's Place
Russell Farms Pumpkin Patch
Sunrise Café at Uptown
Syd's Fine Food and Spirits
Wolfie's Grill

Westfield
Big Hoffa's Barbeque
Erika's Place
Grand Junction Brewing Company Brew Pub
Grand Junction Brewing Company Tap Room
Jan's Village Pizza
J. Razzo's 2
Rail Epicurean Market
Super Bowl Pho
The Italian House on Park
The Local
Titus Bakery at Monon Marketplace
Urban Vines Winery and Brewery
Wolfie's Northern Woods Grill

OTHER HAMILTON COUNTY COMMUNITIES AND BEYOND

Atlanta
Combine Café
Lisa's Pie Shop

Arcadia
Wilson Farm Market

Cicero
10 West
Big Dog's Smokehouse
Cicero Coffee Company
DeLullo's Trattoria

Erika's Place
Titus Bakery

Sheridan
Jan's Village Pizza
Stuckey Farm Market
The Blackhawk Winery and Vineyard

JUST BEYOND HAMILTON COUNTY

Fortville
Foxgardin Kitchen and Ale
Scarlet Lane Brewing Company
Taxman Brewing Company

Perkinsville
Bonge's Tavern

BIBLIOGRAPHY

Chapter 1

Cable.tv. "A History of TV."

Collingham, Lizzie. *The Taste of War*. Penguin Press, 2012.

Culinaryschools.com. September 2013. "What Is the Farm-to-Table Movement?"

Heighway, David. "Enforcing Temperance the Hard Way: Whitecappers Practiced Vigilante Justice." HamiltonCountyBusiness.com.

Morrison, Janelle. "Password Please…A Peek Behind Prohibition." *Towne Post*, 2017.

"Prohibition in 'Bone Dry' Indiana." *Indiana Magazine of History*, December 19, 2011.

"The Road to Prohibition." Indiana Historical Society.

Schumm, Jan. "Food Rationing in Wartime America." History.com, May 23, 2014.

Whitaker, Jan. Foodtimeline.org. 2016.

———. "To Go." Restaurant-ingThroughHistory.com. 2015.

Wikipedia. "Prohibition in the United States." Last edited March 28, 2019, 22:31. https://en.wikipedia.org/wiki/Prohibition_in_the_United_States.

Chapter 2

AtlantaIndiana.com. "Town History."

Greiff, Glory-June. "Official History of Settlement and Life: Sheridan Yesterday and Today." Sheridan Historical Society, 2007.

Heighway, David. "The Great Squirrel Stampede." Highlights in History (blog), Hamilton East Public Library, June 9, 2018. https://www.hepl.lib.in.us/the-great-squirrel-stampede/.

———. "Hamilton County History Timeline." CarmelClayHistory.org.

History of Carmel, Indiana. www.carmel.in.gov.

Van Allen, Elizabeth J. "Carmel Grows Up: The History and Vision of an Edge City." Carmel, IN: Carmel Clay Historical Society, 2017. http://www.carmelclayhistory.org/the-history-of-carmel.

Wikipedia. "Carmel, Indiana." Last edited March 4, 2019, 20:50. https://en.wikipedia.org/wiki/Carmel,_Indiana.

———. "Cicero, Indiana." Last edited March 25, 2019, 9:48. https://en.wikipedia.org/wiki/Cicero,_Indiana.

———. "Fishers, Indiana." Last edited March 27, 2019, 19:46. https://en.wikipedia.org/wiki/Fishers,_Indiana.

———. "1965 Palm Sunday tornado outbreak." Last edited December 7, 2018, 11:08. https://en.wikipedia.org/wiki/1965_Palm_Sunday_tornado_outbreak.

———. "Noblesville, Indiana." Last edited March 20, 2019, 14:55. https://en.wikipedia.org/wiki/Noblesville,_Indiana.

———. "Sheridan, Indiana." Last edited January 27, 2019, 13:36. https://en.wikipedia.org/wiki/Sheridan,_Indiana.

———. "Westfield, Indiana." Last edited February 17, 2019, 18:55. https://en.wikipedia.org/wiki/Westfield,_Indiana.

———. "William Conner." Last edited February 28, 2019, 16:53. https://en.wikipedia.org/wiki/William_Conner.

Chapter 3

Cook, Brad. "Aunt Bee's Fried Chicken." Brad Cook's Hamilton County; *The Times*, November 10, 2014.

———. "Blue Ribbon Dairy 1964." *The Times*, January 1, 2010.

———. "Burger Chef." *The Times*, July 9, 2011.

———. "Clancy's 2004." Brad Cook's Hamilton County; *The Times*. January, 2010.
———. "Original Clancy's." Brad Cook's Hamilton County; *The Times*. June 11, 2012.
———. "Ramsey's Drive-In." Brad Cook's Hamilton County; *The Times*. July 7, 2010.
———. "Wimpy's Grill." Brad Cook's Hamilton County; *The Times*. April 2, 2011.
Couts, Shirley. "Lagoon Lodge: Boxcar Brothel." *The Hamiltonian*. October, 1978.
Hardie, Kevin. "One Dead, Nine Hurt in Building Collapse." *Noblesville Ledger*, February 23, 1977.
Heaton-Snyder, Jerry. "Time for Tea?" *Noblesville Ledger*, March 19, 1991.
Heighway, David. "The 1883 Newspaper War." Hepl.lib.in.us.
Keating, Matt. "Former Owner Recalls Restaurant's Glory Days." *The Daily Ledger*, June 10, 1991.
Reason, Betsy. "The Classic Kitchen's Sale Signals Growth for Cake Baker." *Noblesville Ledger*, September 19, 2007.
Swift, Fred. "Lagoon Lodge a County Secret Site of Note." *The Times*, April 26, 2012.

Chapter 4

Heighway, David. "Helen Cromell AKA 'Dirty Helen.'" Hepl.lib.in.us.

Chapter 6

Kobrowski, Nicole R. *Ghosts of Westfield*. Westfield, IN: Unseen Press, 2011.
Norwalk, K.C. "The Evolution of Indiana's Alcohol Law." Iga.in.gov.

INDEX

ABOUT THE AUTHOR

Photo by Ian Borgerhoff.

Karen Kennedy is an Indianapolis-based writer with a long history in the restaurant business. She once held the job title "Grande Dame" at Chicago's famous Pump Room, which basically meant she was paid to put on rhinestones and schmooze the patrons. She was pretty good at it. She has also worked as a cabaret singer, actress, hand model, advertising copy writer, newspaper reporter, hash slinger, event planner and game show host. When she decides what she wants to be when she grows up, she will get back to you.

Karen is happily married to a brilliant, cello-playing optometrist, her beloved "Peach," Dr. Abigail David, research assistant extraordinaire. On most any weekend, you'll find the two of them in the kitchen cooking up a storm or dining out in one of the Indianapolis area's many fabulous, locally owned restaurants. If you ever find Karen Kennedy in a chain restaurant, call 911, because she has been kidnapped or drugged and left there for dead.